keys to the crystal skulls

divine beacons of light

by Nick Scott-Ram

keys to the crystal skulls

Published by
Lightwork Media
P.O. Box 600
Candler, North Carolina, U.S.A. 28715
1-800-335-1382

Designed by
Paula Chance
Atlanta, Georgia U.S.A.

Library of Congress Catalog Card Number: 2004091590
Scott-Ram, Nick. 2004
ISBN 1-887343-85-7

Printed in the United State of America.
First Printing 2004
10   9   8   7   6   5   4   3   2   1

Dedication

To Frances
True love in a star

Front Cover Painting

By Cornelia Selkirk

Contents

List of Meditations

Synopsis

The second volume in the *Keys* series, *Keys to the Crystal Skulls. Divine Beacons of Light* describes the core role that the crystal skulls will play in the new evolution of humanity into the Sixth Root Race. The crystal skulls are beacons of Divine Light at their highest and purest level: they act as Divine amplifiers to a host of crystalline energies, and are Divine creators of reality. They can be accessed in the physical realms, for instance through the Mitchell-Hedges crystal skull, or on the inner planes through meditation. *Keys to the Crystal Skulls* describes how to access their different frequencies, and how to work with different types of crystalline energy, such as crystalline guides, that can be presented within our awareness. By building an inner crystalline bridge of light between our outer physical body and our inner higher awareness, it becomes possible to access a vast array of crystalline energies within.

Keys to the Crystal Skulls also describes some of the history of the crystal skulls in energetic terms, in relation to the previous root races, such as the Lemurian and Atlanean Root Races. The skulls have a central role in the new root race, and specific ones will be brought into play that will download a massive array of new, Divine Frequencies. These include the energies of the Cosmic Christ that will generate a massive ascendancy of frequencies in humanity; the accessing of new star-maps through stellar cartography; the formation of new blends of energy, such as angelic-crystalline frequencies that will be housed in the physical spaces of the new children; a connection with other crystal skulls, such as the Dolphin-Oceanic skull; and the seeding of new crystalline beacons within our awareness, with crystalline acorns.

As the Sixth Root Race unfolds, the crystal skulls will usher in a new kind of soul light that will lead to the merging of hearts and minds of different soul aspects, and souls throughout the planet. As souls begin to merge in harmony, and to create a new breed of soul mate, humanity will enjoy a new type of love, formed within the heart, that will quite literally, take the breath away. As this ascension takes place, a much more direct bridge will be established with our higher selves, and ultimately with our true inner divinity. This whole process will reflect the unfolding of the Sixth Root Race as ordained by the Avatar of the Age, Meher Baba.

Keys to the Crystal Skulls provides the reader with practical meditations to connect directly with the crystal skulls, and sets out in detail some of the energetic changes that are upon us now, and will remain for many years to come. It portrays a rich and deep energetic interpretation of the crystal skulls and their associated crystalline energies.

Acknowledgements

There are a number of people who deserve special mention in the preparation of this book. First and foremost is David Cousins, whose divine teaching over the years and beyond, continues to peel off layer upon layer of reality, inner and outer, and has helped me, beyond words, to provide an informational and light base that is the inspiration for the work. His light and love show me the way. Second is my wife Frances, who has shown me true love, and is an inspiration to draw upon. For her love, support and encouragement, I owe a deep debt of gratitude and my love.

I also owe a large debt to Cornelia Selkirk, for the work we have done together over the years involving crystalline energy. It has been utterly invaluable in the drawing together of sections of this book. I would also like to thank her for providing the wonderful painting for the cover. A big thank you to Vaune Newcomb-Hodgetts, who kindly commented on early drafts and whose heartfelt input provided a great inspiration in the writing process. Her participation was invaluable.

There are others with whom I have shared a number of different experiences and discussions as part of the book's evolution. Principally these have been friends in workshops, and while there are too many of them to include all the names here, I would like to record the debt of gratitude that is owed for the work that we have done together. Hopefully, you know who you are.

I would like to thank Trish Miller for her work in the editing process. Editing a book of this type is not an easy process, and I have greatly valued her consideration and careful work. I would also like to say a big thank you to Lily WhiteRose at LightWork Media in the publication of this book, and for her support in this project. It is deeply appreciated.

Chapter 1 • Introduction

*K*eys to the Crystal Skulls: Beacons of Divine Light is the second book in a series entitled *Keys*. The first book, *Keys to our Heart: A Prelude to the Sixth Root Race*, presents a series of new frequencies of light that can be accessed primarily through the heart centre or chakra. The particular focus of these light frequencies is love, and *Keys to Our Heart* is an introduction to connecting with these different love vibrations and their role in the beginning of the Sixth Root Race. While the Sixth Root Race may be a new concept to many people, its origins and reference point can be found in many spiritual writings. It is the emerging root race which is succeeding the Fifth, or Aryan, Root Race. The root races represent an expression of form in matter according to Divine Will, and as the Fifth comes to an end, and the Sixth fires up, a significant shift in the vibration and consciousness of the human race will be necessary. This shift will be accompanied by a dramatic change in frequency vibration throughout the Planet: it will impact upon all life forms, be they mineral, plant, animal or human. High-frequency light, and new love vibrations founded on unconditional love, will form the building blocks of this massive shift.

Among the primary conduits for shaping this new consciousness and view of reality are the crystal skulls. I am not referring to any old, skull-shaped, crystal artefact that has been formed and shaped from minerals. The crystal skulls which are the focus of this book are those artefacts which are principally formed of quartz, and which have a signal or vibration of great purity and beauty, as well as the potential to act as spiritual generators. Two of the best-known examples are the Mitchell-Hedges crystal skull and the British Museum crystal skull, both of which radiate a vibration of sufficient quality to set them apart from the majority of other crystal skulls. Indeed, many of those to be found in collections house much lower frequencies. They are therefore not the subject of this book.

The aim here is to describe some of the roles of crystal skulls as spiritual generators and amplifiers; in order to help the reader establish a direct connection with the new frequencies, and ultimately to access new levels of crystalline information. While this can be done through physical contact, the crystal skulls can easily be accessed internally, without a physical reference point. Apart from discussing the important role that the crystal skulls will play in the forthcoming emergence of the Sixth Root Race, this book will also cover ways of accessing crystalline frequencies in general, and how to build an internal crystalline hologram that can house them.

In contrast to *Keys to the Heart*, which focuses on the heart and its role as a doorway, *Keys to the Crystal Skulls* is centred more explicitly on the third eye, which functions as a new doorway to the higher crystalline frequencies. Although the same can be said of the heart centre, there is a difference between these two chakras in terms of the types of frequency that can be accessed. Nevertheless, both the heart chakra and the third eye can function as dimensional doorways to different dimensional spaces, and have an extremely important role to play in the evolution of the Sixth Root Race. As a prerequisite to this evolutionary shift, both centres need to be cleared and stripped of older subliminal frequencies that can be a hindrance to fully effective functioning. Older chordings relating to past-life happenings also need to be stripped away, and the internal space of both of these chakra centres in particular needs to be significantly expanded, for the initial sequence of the Sixth Root Race will require such an expansion, followed by an energetic interplay between the two centres.

Initially the heart centre will begin to move up into the third eye. As this movement gathers momentum, ultimately the heart centre will be able to be housed at will within the third eye. This will require a significant expansion of the third eye centre, and it will open up a more telepathic pathway between people working in this way. In a very real sense it will be like experiencing a heart 'love' connection in the third eye, representing a much deeper linking with all that is around. So while it is something of an over-simplification to say that the principal focus of this book is on the third eye, whereas in *Keys to Our Heart* the focus was on the heart centre, the interplay between these two chakras will be just as important as their burgeoning expansion, and the housing of new frequencies within both. At the same time, it is important to recognise that many of the crystalline frequencies mentioned here have, as their starting mechanism, a connection with the divinity of the heart.

Although the Sixth Root Race is concerned with the ascending frequencies of love and light, another aspect is the diversity and beauty of our crystalline heritage. There is tremendous excitement on the inner planes at the prospect of this new unfolding. A huge wave of crystalline energy is bearing down on us, ready to enfold, merge with and raise our vibration to new spheres of previously undreamed exquisiteness. What is happening now is a culmination of all that has gone before, and those on the inner planes have had to wait a long time for this new dawn. Now that it is moving towards us at high speed, it is up to us to grab this new opportunity with love and joy. The crystalline energies will accept nothing less.

My own introduction to the crystal skulls occurred during meditation. I was on a David Cousins course in Majorca, and early one morning I decided to sit in the meditation room and open up to the energies around. After a period, as I opened my eyes, I saw the image of a clear, crystal skull measuring approximately 1.5-2 metres from the tip of the occiput to the front of the upper jaw. The skull, which was rotating rapidly around a central vertical axis, moved into the centre of the room for a few seconds and then disappeared. It was a somewhat odd sight, but at the same time most beautiful. While not all the features of the skull were visible to me, the crystalline outline, and the transparent and translucent quality within, were clear. After this initial experience, I was fortunate enough to see first the British Museum crystal skull and then the Mitchell-Hedges crystal skull in the physical.

The British Museum skull was housed in the Museum of Mankind in London until several years ago. Standing in front of it, it was very obvious to me that there was an energy charge pulsing from it: and in opening myself up to the skull I felt as if my energy signal became more refined, condensed and focused upwards. As time went by, I could feel strong pulsations in my third eye. I visited this skull on several occasions, and always experienced a similar, powerful effect. Following this, there was, in February 1998, a public viewing of the Mitchell-Hedges crystal skull in Torquay, Devon, by Anna Mitchell-Hedges, combined with a talk by David Cousins about the skull. The energy and focus of this one was more refined than that in the British Museum, and apart from its physical beauty and purity, it was clear it was also more active.

Following on from these experiences, I began to build a stronger inner-planes connection with the crystal skulls. One of the most vivid experiences I had was during a workshop meditation, in which I found myself going down the stairs into an ancient temple. It felt most strongly Egyptian, with tall columns on either side, and rows of hieroglyphics on the walls. As I went down into a large stone chamber, I was drawn to some doors on the other side of the temple. I went through them into a dark corridor that eventually came out into a small dark chamber via another set of doors. I was confronted by a most beautiful sight — a completely clear quartz crystal skull, of about the same dimensions as the Mitchell-Hedges skull in real life, but subtly different in appearance. The skull hung in the air at head height, and had a brilliant internal light. As I looked into the crystalline eye sockets, I heard a voice in my head, stating that the crystal skull was mine. My inner response was that I did not own the skull, and that it was for humanity. After this inner exchange, I felt the skull come towards me and then merge with my head. It was an extraordinarily physical and powerful experience. The feeling of love that overwhelmed me was also most intense, as both my third eye and my heart felt the crystalline skull energy most strongly.

These initial experiences were an introduction to the beauty, love and power of the crystal skulls. Since that time, I have worked with them on the inner planes in a variety of ways, focusing on different crystal skulls and building deeper connections with them through merging exercises involving different chakra centres. This book draws on those experiences, and aims to give the reader an opportunity to access these divine, crystalline, light frequencies in a meaningful and direct way. The quantity and quality of information that is held within these different crystal skulls is awesome, and it is available in varying degrees to those who have the perseverance, love and understanding to establish a true link with them. I very much hope that this book may contribute in some small way to facilitating this link, and to providing a glimpse of what the crystal skulls represent in today's new dawn.

The first part of the book focuses on crystalline energies: how to access them, what they represent, and how they form part of an ancient heritage within each of us that was present before we incarnated into physical matter. These crystalline realms represent a different level of awareness and consciousness. Ways of recognising and accessing higher levels of crystalline guidance also form an important component in accessing a better energetic understanding of crystalline frequencies and the nature of crystalline reality.

Following on from this informational grounding in crystalline energies, the next section covers the crystal skulls: it includes the diversity of their frequencies; their origins; how to access them and build up an ongoing dialogue with them through merging; and ultimately forging an inner crystalline bridge with them. There are many different crystal skulls that can be accessed, each of which houses a host of sublime light frequencies. Information on how to access this array through meditation is also included.

This platform of energetic interchange forms the basis for the subsequent sections of the book, including a series of more focused channellings: on crystal skull formation; on their role in relation to the different root races, in particular to Lemurian and Atlantean times; and on how the skulls can be used to provide information on new star maps which are beginning to seed the consciousness of those open to the changes demanded by the Sixth Root Race. These maps have particularly important roles associated with the new babies being birthed into the Planet. There is also a description of the new wave of crystalline energy that will be manifested by the Cosmic Christ as part of the ascendancy of energies entering the Planet.

A further section deals with different ways of working with the crystal skulls, and using them as a seeding mechanism for new information. This seeding mechanism is part of the forerunner of a new crystalline grid of energy that is being established around the Planet, and which will act as an energetic transmitter and conductor to higher, extra-terrestrial frequencies. This seeding will be spectacular and dynamic in its effects. The crystal skulls have a central role to play in bringing into matter the Sixth Root Race thought-form: they will help to bring through a range of new frequencies which will be stunning in their beauty, and which will, quite literally, restructure and re-align humanity in an entirely new way.

The last part of the book focuses on the crystalline frequencies in relation to the heart, so that there is a change in emphasis and blending between third eye and heart. Ultimately, this development will transform the energetic interplay between our heart centres and our third eyes, and the new crystalline frequencies will reflect this massive shift.

Much of the information contained in this book was channelled, and therefore contains specific overtones in relation to different levels of information, and new frequencies. This means that certain passages may not appear to make any logical sense, and I would strongly urge you not to attempt to focus *intellectually* on these sections. The overtone that arises from this material contains within it specific frequencies that will activate different centres, both subconsciously and consciously, as part of the downloading of crystalline energy into the subtle anatomy. The intention is to introduce you to different crystalline codes of access to new internal doorways, while providing a collective platform for greater unity and harmony within the planet.

It is therefore easier to *feel* the energy and information contained within this book, and to accept that not all of it will make intellectual sense. It is also helpful to trust that there is an inherent intuitive feel, or energetic pulse, that will provide you with all that it is necessary for you to access.

Different people will resonate with this book in different ways, dependent upon their past evolution into matter, and whether they have had any past-life connections with the crystal skulls. Some connections will have been dormant for some considerable time, and the reconnection with some of the new frequencies may be extremely subtle. Some readers may have had close connections with the crystal skulls in past lives, acting as keepers, and for them the connection may consequently feel more profound. However, it is worth remembering that whatever your past-life connection with the crystal skulls, the energies today represent a new start for all of us. The new crystalline energies are high-frequency. The higher the vibration, the more subtle it is, and so just because something is not *felt*, does not mean that there is no connection. Practice, and the reinforcing of the crystalline connections will slowly strip away the veils from the past, and will ultimately allow new frequencies to be housed in a more tangible and direct way.

As in *Keys to Our Heart*, certain sections of text are italicised and indented. These sections are direct channellings from crystalline guides, and are designed to provide an access point or doorway. The vibration embodied in these sections will help give you a recognition signal, and an alignment with crystalline energy. Again, these sections should not be approached from an intellectual perspective.

A short glossary of terms has been included, to help give the reader a background on some of the topics and issues raised in the book. The glossary complements some of the definitions given in the main text, and also provides further information on essential background areas.

Finally, it only remains for me to stress that the information and frequencies contained in this book are an interpretation of the new energies. As with all aspects of life, there is a constant flux, and I hope that some of the frequencies expressed in these pages will resonate with you in some way. The guidance behind them reflects a profound love of humanity.

The aim of this chapter is to provide the reader with a brief but comprehensive introduction to different crystalline frequencies. We shall explore the nature of these frequencies, providing a short summary of some of the different types that are accessible to us, including the crystal skulls. This will be followed by a short résumé on working with physical crystals. Much has been written about physical crystals in other books, and the aim is not to duplicate this. The main emphasis will be upon the importance of working with pure crystals. We shall then focus on the formation of our own crystalline light body: this can be initiated as a crystalline thought-form, which can subsequently be constructed to house and connect with an array of crystalline frequencies. The final part of this chapter will focus on a brief description of the crystalline realms or spheres.

Crystalline Frequencies

The crystalline frequencies now entering the Planet represent a new dawn in terms of energetic manifestation: they are a manifestation of specific light frequencies, originating in the higher planes, (especially the fifth, sixth and seventh), which have been dormant for long periods of time. The time has come for their reactivation and this process is now in full flow. Crystalline frequencies, as described in this book, represent a new matrix of alignment underpinned by will and intent. This means that the application of will (which fuels intent), when focused in the crystalline realms, can open new doorways to crystalline frequencies of massive diversity, and exquisite beauty. These new frequencies, which contain within them a substantial source of information on matters crystalline, and on their relevance to planetary evolution at this time, represent a significant opportunity to re-open old doorways, and to build major new portals of light. The irradiation of crystalline frequencies into the planet is now activating those light workers and others who have a sympathetic alignment with such frequencies: those people who can recognise the crystalline song, who can respond to it, open up to it within their awareness, and subsequently earth the new frequencies within their own bodies. Generally, this recognition is born of past-life work with crystalline energy, which for many light workers dates back to Lemurian and Atlantean time periods, as representations of the Third and Fourth Root Races respectively.

For many people, crystalline frequencies are understood in terms of grosser physical objects which, while interesting in their own right, do not do full justice to the true diversity of crystalline energies. The analogy is rather similar to that of an iceberg, where the physical reference points are represented by the visible tip of the iceberg, while the true scope and diversity of crystalline energies relate to that which is generally hidden, i.e. by far the greater portion. One of the main purposes of this book is to introduce the reader to this 'hidden' portion. It remains true, of course, that physical crystals can act as excellent reference points and starting mechanisms for accessing the new frequencies. Just as physical crystals have their own internal geometry and physical properties that define their shape, size and colour, and their ability to contain and transmit light, so the crystalline frequencies on the inner planes have their own internal geometry of light.

The true extent of crystalline energies housed on the inner planes is staggering: it is beyond the scope of the normal limitations of the mind. The crystalline energies cover a vast ocean of frequencies in multi-dimensional inner space. This range of frequencies is massive, spanning the fifth, sixth and seventh planes and beyond. Imagine if you will, a giant crystalline "piano", with millions upon millions of notes, rather than just the original 88; each note reflecting a crystalline frequency, and possessing its own energy focus and harmonic. Within each note, further sub-divisions or refinements of crystalline vibration are also possible, so that the permutations of notes that can be played are almost limitless within a crystalline context. The beauty of each crystalline note is also, quite literally, out of this world. Each note has a resonance, purity and clarity of energy. Each is like a crystalline string, which can be played on the winds of timelessness; and each can forge a new essence of light and love within our own consciousness. Within the "piano", some notes can be accessed through the fifth plane, some from the sixth, and others from the seventh. It is as if the base notes are found in the fifth plane, the middle notes in the sixth, and the higher ones in the seventh.

Taking this analogy one stage further, the combination of notes and formation of chords can be likened to the crystal skulls themselves. Each skull will be a combination of crystalline notes; in some cases just a few notes, and in others a broader array. Or to put it another way, the crystal skulls may reflect specific octaves of notes which can be played within different scales, such as B flat, C major, and so on. The scale will reflect the underlying crystalline focus, as manifest through intent and will, while the range of notes included will cover the bandwidth or scope of reality that the crystal skull will invoke.

The notes on the crystalline "piano" therefore reflect the diversity of frequencies that can be accessed within the crystalline realms. The "piano" itself, which is also made of crystal, is the underlying matrix or grid of Divine Light that supports the crystalline frequencies. The piano Player is God Himself or, as He is known in the current Avataric age, Meher Baba. As Meher Baba plays these notes, different sets of crystalline energies are activated, and are seeded into the appropriate plane level for access by the various life forms, including humanity. Different crystal skulls can become activated by the Divine music. And as the Divine Father plays, He looks with intent, will and love at the sole crystal skull that is set atop the crystalline "piano", directly in front of Him: the skull upon which He is focusing at that particular point.

Crystalline frequencies can therefore only be truly accessed from the higher planes, namely the mental planes and beyond. Whole crystalline worlds exist in different dimensions populated by crystalline life forms and intelligences, where both solid and liquid crystal are found. These are worlds of exquisite beauty, and we shall explore how to access some of them through working with crystalline guides. One of the manifestations of the building of bridges with the crystalline worlds will be the earthing of the new frequencies into the planet, so that — quite literally — crystalline cities will be present in selected power spots around the globe. Principal amongst these is the crystalline city at Seclusion Hill in India, which is where Meher Baba did much of His Divine Work in isolation from humanity.

Apart from presenting new dimensional doorways to other worlds, crystalline frequencies will also open up a new understanding of what we are and where we have come from. This illumination will reveal an aspect of our soul's divine journey: from initial separation from God, down through the gaseous, angelic and crystalline realms into physical matter, to the return journey in physical form — back into God. Connecting with our ancient crystalline heritage forms a unique part of this process, as we can chart our journey through the crystalline realms: a journey which truly defines our crystalline essence.

The crystal skulls also have an extremely important role to play in the birthing of the Sixth Root Race. They act as seeding mechanisms for crystalline worlds on the inner planes, and if we commune with them they will facilitate direct access to these inner dimensions. Beyond that, the crystal skulls are housing-mechanisms for the creation of new realities in both subtle and physical form.

In the birthing of the Sixth Root Race, crystalline energy will play an important role in transforming our physical bodies to handle and hold the range of new frequencies available, because as we wake up to what is on offer, our bodies also will have to change. The change will be a dramatic one: it will demand that old, slow frequencies (i.e. those held in from the past) be removed, and that the electronic foundations of our energetic systems be completely overhauled. This will be somewhat analogous to the complete rewiring of a house. All of the old wiring and switches first have to be stripped out, and then new maps for upgraded electronic wiring must be introduced, followed by the actual rewiring process itself. The choice of material for this "rewiring" will also be important, and will comprise ascending frequencies of light: crystalline light and other types of light. The process will vary from individual to individual — in some it will be subtle, in others more physical and ruthless. Another feature of the "rewiring" is that it is an ongoing process. Multiple repetitions will occur, to accompany and reflect the increasing vibratory patterns of energy being fed into our systems. Each rewiring will be more refined than the previous one, and will allow a greater capacity to connect with and house the higher-frequency energies. This stepping-stone process will ensure that our systems can cope with the new energies, and that we don't 'fuse' our electrical circuitry or 'blow' our chakra centres.

Our bodies will need to be rewired at every level — physical, etheric, astral and mental — and the process will involve a diversity of different energetic inputs, including that of crystalline energy. This process will lead to the generation of a crystalline matrix of light contained within our physical shells. This matrix will be of liquid crystal, and will act as a transceiver and storage device of new crystalline frequencies. It will look like a clear crystalline body, which can function separately from the physical body, and ultimately be used as a vehicle of crystalline consciousness.

The manifestation of crystalline intent will bring about a transformation in the new vibrations that will be housed within the Planet. These vibrations will represent a new seeding mechanism of crystalline energy, and as the seeds are planted in the garden of humanity, then new crystalline trees of great majesty and beauty will grow; trees which will form part of the matrix of crystalline energies that will envelop Earth and contribute to its massive vibrational shift. This crystalline grid will not be restricted to the planet Earth. The frequencies and energies housed within it will be radiated outwards to other planets and solar systems, ultimately impacting upon the other 18,000 earths that form the wheel of life, from the outer rim of the universe to our Earth at its centre.

As this crystalline energy is pushed out into the universe as a wave of high-frequency light energy, other life forms will be affected by it, and will respond to it. The crystalline matrix will be like an invocation, an invitation to turn to the new Sixth Root Race light, offering these other life forms the opportunity to plug into this high-frequency grid. The results will be spectacular for all concerned.

In all, the birthing of new crystalline frequencies in the Planet will ensure that things will never be the same again. Just as humanity will be deeply affected by the changes, so will the mineral, plant and animal kingdoms. All will evolve to a higher frequency, and will receive infusions of crystalline energy. The minerals themselves will be able to house greater quantities of high-frequency crystalline energy leading to a shift in the frequency of the ground energies. As these then increase their vibration, old and more recently-stored slow-frequency energy will of necessity be released in the time-honoured fashion of earth movements and other physical disturbances. Thus will the changes affecting humanity be reflected throughout the Planet.

Throughout all of this, humanity will be building a deeper dialogue with the inner crystalline worlds and life forms. As the downloading of crystalline frequencies from the higher planes becomes more intense, our sense of inner and outer reality will change. We shall be standing at one moment in the world, and at the next we shall feel as if we are somewhere entirely different; such as a crystalline world, where the colours and sensations feel strange and wondrous, but nonetheless real. These feelings will be like the unlocking of the new crystalline frequencies, or more accurately, specific frequency notes that embody a rich vein of light energy and information: and the feelings will become more common, and more intense.

So, to summarise, the new crystalline frequencies entering the Planet represent a unique opportunity for us to access new dimensional doorways of light and love, and to build a divine inner pathway to new vistas of crystalline light. There is a wealth of crystalline frequencies available to humanity at this time, and as we invoke them, and ground them within our physical vehicles, significant and permanent changes will take place in both our reality and our understanding of who we are.

Working with Physical Crystals

For many people, the easiest way to begin to access these new crystalline frequencies is to work with physical crystals. It is commonly recognised that so many of the building-blocks of our planet, and of many other worlds, are based on crystals. Each type of crystal has its own signature and its own capacity to contain and radiate light, plus unique sets of other properties; and although this physical manifestation is but a shadowy reflection of the reality of whole realms of crystalline energy and crystalline worlds on the inner planes, working with physical crystals can help us to build up a rapport with the crystalline energy.

The focus of any crystalline work is to access the higher-frequency crystalline energies. This effectively means tuning in to the mental vibrations, rather than to those which have been stepped down into the lower planes, including the astral levels. In tuning in to these higher frequencies, physical crystals can be used as symbolic reference points and energetic doorways.

The choice of crystalline object is extremely important. Light workers often use crystals as physical reference points, but this is not always necessary, and it can be a hindrance if the crystals utilised are not of a sufficiently high frequency. Crystals will reflect their place of origin, the energies they have been associated with, and what they have picked up from their environment. It is therefore essential to select crystals with a higher vibration, and which have been thoroughly cleansed, blessed and dedicated. Provided crystals of great purity and high vibration are selected, then they can act as doorways to different dimensional realms of crystalline energy, and provide support structures for new levels of guidance to enter our space.

Before working with any crystal, it is important to *intuit* its feel — its vibration. This can be done by sensing what happens when you intuitively place your energy in the crystal. Does your vibration go up or down? What happens to your frequency signal? Does it become narrower and more refined, or broader and more dispersed? Each crystal will have its own signature tune, which once identified is easy to recognise. Divining crystals in this simple way can help you to recognise your energetic connection with them, and to assess whether or not a specific crystal is appropriate for your energy system.

When tuning in to a high vibration, pure quartz crystal can act as a starting-point for the process. There is a smoothness, a coolness and a liquid sense of purity embodied in such crystals, and while it may be possible to sense other vibrations in them, it is worth building up a sense of what crystalline energy feels like. This recognition pattern can then be used as a yardstick by which to gauge other crystalline frequencies as you encounter them on the inner planes. It is also worth remembering that different people will have different connections with a particular crystal. For one person a crystal may feel intuitively 'right' to work with, while for another it does not. Practising connecting with and feeling crystalline energy in physical crystalline objects is a useful starting point. Proper steps to protect and clear your energy system should be taken when doing this kind of work.

The meditation below is a straightforward way to clear a crystal of any unwanted energies. Initially, it is also helpful to clean crystals in salty water for over 24 hours, so that any superficial slow-frequency energies can be removed. An array of other techniques is to be found in *A Handbook for Light Workers*.

Meditation to Bless and Dedicate a Crystal

First connect with the Paramatman Light, the Divine Light which passes all understanding, and which is accessed on the seventh plane. Bring this Light down into your whole body, filling up all the chakra centres. Once this has been done, place a shamanistic robe of crystalline light around the whole of your body, sealing up your aura — this will prevent any unwanted energies from entering your system and acts as a protective mechanism. You can then either place your hands around the crystal or set it in front of you, and imagine that a circle of blue light surrounds it. See the crystal in the centre of this blue circle, and then within the circle visualise a golden triangle. The crystal should also sit inside this triangle. Now superimpose a white rose over the crystal, and allow the rose to change colour. This is an intuitive process, and it is important to trust your initial impressions. Just allow whatever comes to you to be accepted. Typically, in impure crystals the rose will change to a dark colour, grey or brown. Feel during this process the Paramatman Light beginning to flow out through your hands into the crystal. This downloading of energy helps to drive the colour changes in the rose, which may stay dark for several minutes or longer, or may change colour to something a little lighter. Eventually the rose should turn back to pure white. Once this has taken place, the crystal will have been blessed and dedicated. It will also be more in tune with your own energy system. Depending on how pure you feel your crystal is, the above procedure can be repeated as often as you intuitively feel is appropriate.

Crystalline Light Bodies

The crystalline light body is a frequency resonator which surrounds the physical body. It is a vehicle of consciousness, and has a separate reality and composition from the physical body. In appearance, it is shaped like the human body, but is several inches larger all the way round. The light body is made up of an exquisite intermeshing of crystalline frequencies, representing previous interactions with crystalline light, as manifested in different past incarnations. It provides a reference point for the new wave of crystalline energy entering the Planet. Everyone who is working with crystalline energies will develop a crystalline light body, the formation of which will be dependent upon the individual's intensity of focus and access to crystalline frequencies. The broader and deeper the connection, the more intense will be the crystalline light body. The formation of the light body will take time: it will be established over months and years of intensive work with crystalline frequencies.

Once a basic pattern for the crystalline light body has been set down, it can function in a number of different ways. It will pulse and glow in response to varied inputs of crystalline energy, which will wash through the crystalline light body and become absorbed within it. The frequency level will vary in response to the degree of refinement or type of incoming crystalline energy. High-frequency crystalline light will only be 'captured' by a very refined crystalline light body, one that vibrates at a high enough level to contain such frequencies. Thus the crystalline light body will act as a tuning-fork to different crystalline vibrations, and it is the scope or flexibility of the light body that will determine the types of frequency that can be held or attained to. The greater the scope, the more varied the types of crystalline frequency that can be absorbed. The narrower the focus, the more specialised the light body.

Initially, the crystalline light body may only partially cover the physical body, so that a portion of leg or arm or face will reflect the crystalline input. The main impediment to the formation of the light body is the presence of old, dark frequencies trapped within the physical and etheric vehicles. These old frequencies, which reflect past-life experiences where dark intent dominated, must be flushed out of the system, so that they can be replaced with light frequencies. It is rather like having a patchwork appearance to the body, which is made up of small patches, both dark and light. These patches can be represented in different ways, for example as feathers, crystals or snowflakes. Each will represent a lifetime focused in light or darkness, and it is only through the cleansing or purification of these past lives that the vibrational patchwork can be transformed overall into light frequencies. In addition, the number of feathers or crystals will relate to the number of lives spent in matter. For the old soul, this will converge on the average of 8,400,000 lives required to experience the full diversity of frequencies, and to balance all levels of karma. Young and "middle-aged" souls will have been through a lesser complement of lives, and will reflect this in the development of their light bodies.

A key aspect of the new root race is collective focus. What this means is that if we work in isolation or as individuals, then it will be impossible to achieve what is being demanded of us. Our focus has to be collective i.e. group-orientated. This is important in all that we do, especially in our energy work: collectively shared meditations and other energy exercises can be much more powerful than those performed in isolation. This sense of working collectively is important to the stripping away of the old, and its replacement by the new. In a group setting, past lives can be worked through and released much more rapidly than through individual efforts. It has to be recognised, though, that working with a physical group may not always be possible, and so focusing with collective intent in meditations and other forms of energy work is especially useful. To call in all light workers, or "the group" during meditations is a meaningful reflection of the collective need.

As each life is spun through energy-management of the group collective, it is possible to build, quite rapidly, a light body of exquisite light frequencies. Dark frequencies need to be surrendered to the group collective, and this is largely an unconscious process. While this change can be invoked in practice, it is only through management of energies within a group context that it can be achieved most effectively. So rather than working to clear one or two dark frequencies representing a life or two, the focus should be on clearing and offering up slow frequencies from tens of thousands of lives; and even hundreds of thousands of lives. As this process develops, the frequency range that can be entertained by the crystalline light body will be greatly enhanced, and the signal generated will ascend accordingly.

Group management of these crystalline frequencies is therefore very significant. Recognising and connecting with crystalline light bodies in other light workers is important, and it can provide a principle focus for exchanging frequencies, and clearing old ones. In this process, dark frequencies are offered up to the group, and then spun within a group energy format, before being released as light frequencies. Effectively the dark is transmuted and digested by the energy system of the group members, and then the light frequencies are released. This transmutation is an ongoing process in any group setting, and the efficiency and effectiveness depend upon the 'voltage' of the group, the collective degree of previous lives in light or dark, and upon its will and intent to achieve the goal.

Meditation to Build a Crystalline Light Body

This meditation can be done in conjunction with the 'Connecting with Crystalline Guides Meditation' described in Chapter 4. As a developing pattern you may find it easier to work with that meditation first, and then to build upon that platform using this meditation:

Clear your mind, and allow your body to settle into silence. Call upon the Paramatman Light, the Light source from the seventh plane, to enter your space. Since energy follows thought, this procedure and invocation will begin to establish a connection with the Paramatman Light. Allow the Light to stream down into your crown, filling the whole of your body, and all of the chakra centres. Then cloak yourself in a protective robe of crystalline light, imagining every part of your body surrounded by it. The robe should be firmly done up at the front: its purpose is to protect your system from any negative or loose energy that would be detrimental to your energy work, and it effectively seals off your aura. Then call in the group of light workers working for the Divine Plan. The group can be represented as a brilliant white or golden disc that is placed in the heart centre. This will connect you energetically with the group or collective.

Once these initial procedures have been completed, send out a call for your highest crystalline guides. Feel this guidance coming up behind you, and imagine large crystalline figures — three to four metres high — standing there. Ask for any negative energies to be cleared from within your internal and external space. Focus then on the bones in your body, directing the Paramatman Light into them. Fill first the inside of bone, then the bone itself with Light, and then allow the Light to fill up the internal organs, muscles, connective tissue, and ultimately your skin. Take time to do this until the whole of your body is filled with the Paramatman Light. You should feel calm, relaxed, centred, at peace with yourself.

Then expand the Light to several inches off the body, thus building a light body which is several inches bigger overall than your physical body. It will feel as if this body is bigger, but is made up entirely of high-frequency light. Once this is done, and again take time to do this, begin to project all of your awareness into this light body, until it feels more 'real' than your physical body. As your awareness fills the light body, it will be as if it has an independent awareness of its own. Once you feel confident that you have done this, imagine the light body standing up and walking towards the centre of the room you are in. Once in the centre, turn around in your light body, and look back at yourself sitting in meditation.

Maintaining your focus may take some practice. If you feel that your awareness remains within your physical body rather than in the crystalline body, repeat the process with several crystalline bodies, building each of them up, and then walking into the centre of the room. With practice, you will be able to transfer a greater and greater amount of your awareness into your crystalline body, where to the point you will be more in the crystalline body than the physical one.

Once you have been to the centre of the room in your crystalline body, slowly walk back towards your physical body, then turn around and sit back down into your physical shell. Feel again your light body being slightly larger than your physical body, and then begin to move your awareness back from the light body into your physical one. Once this is complete, contract the light body back into the physical.

To complete the meditation, it is important to close your chakra centres and slow down your vibration by making your shamanistic robe heavier and darker.

The above process is a starting-mechanism, and once you begin to work more closely with your crystalline guides, you can bring through high-frequency crystalline light as the building-blocks for your crystalline light robe. It is important to be aware that this meditation will use up large quantities of pranic energy, and so you may feel tired after it. This tiredness is due in part to the stripping away of older frequencies, and to the formation of a new thought form that requires the input of high-frequency crystalline light.

With time and patience, and through working in a collective mode, it is possible to build crystalline light bodies of sufficient purity and strength to begin to access and hold in the physical the new crystalline frequencies. The crystalline light body will radiate high-frequency light, and will store and reflect higher crystalline vibrations, which will be part of the collective association of crystalline energies. By building and connecting with the crystalline light body, it will be possible to feel one's awareness as a crystalline being. The feeling is one of deep quiet, depth, peace and stillness, which radiates or permeates throughout the crystalline matrix of the light body. By becoming aware of this body, you can directly access higher crystalline frequencies, and raise your vibration to match those of the mental planes. The crystalline light body will also have a feeling of liquidity and coolness, so that your awareness permeates it, and it is possible to scan for areas of slower frequency, or those that need to be irradiated with crystalline light. Connection with the crystalline light body can form the basis for accessing a diversity of frequencies, so that as each frequency is downloaded into the light body, it can be lived or experienced within a crystalline medium. This also provides an alternative reference point to the normal physical body, where a crystalline body can be experienced as something separate yet equally real.

Within the process of crystallization, the chakras also have to change, and to become doorways for crystalline energy. Just as the light body must be cleansed and purified of slower frequencies, the chakras must go through a similar process of dredging and releasing old frequencies. Once cleansed to a reasonable degree, each chakra will provide in itself an access point to crystalline energy. For most light workers, this will focus primarily through the third eye and heart chakras, and to a lesser extent the throat chakra. However, it is important not to forget the lower chakras, for the solar plexus and sexual centres will both play an important role in acting as a platform for the higher energies. Clearing these lower chakras is important, since they will provide a strong balancing mechanism for the holding of higher-frequency energy. One way of assessing the degree of light or dark crystalline energy in each centre is to mentally place a crystal in each centre and visualise whether it becomes light or dark. This can then act as a reference point for further clearing. It is important to remember that clearing the chakras will require multiple sessions, since residues of old energies will be retained from multiple past lives.

Once this process is complete, it will be possible to start working with the crystalline light body in new ways. At one level, the crystalline light body is a vehicle of consciousness and experience, and can be projected through intent and focus to different places both on the inner and physical planes. In particular, you can develop your crystalline body as a parallel, or super-charged version of the astral body. Whereas the astral body allows primary access to the astral planes, and cannot travel up into the higher ones, the crystal body has direct access to the mental planes and can be used as a vehicle of higher consciousness.

Within the physical, the light body can be invoked to resonate with high-vibration energy spots on the Planet, such as Seclusion Hill in India, and to act as a reservoir for high-frequency energy. On the inner planes, conscious projection of the crystalline light body into the mental planes and into the crystalline spheres can open up new doorways to different worlds. By resonating at the same frequency within the crystalline light body as that which can be found in the higher mental planes, different degrees of energetic merging can take place, such as with crystalline guides, with the crystal skulls, or with other crystalline energies. The greater the merging, the more the energy that is downloaded, and the higher the vibration that is embedded within the crystalline light body. This process of downloading and digesting higher crystalline frequencies will directly impact upon the physical body, as appearance, organs, body shape and bones will begin to reflect the new crystalline patterns.

Within the physical body, the bones represent the most direct connection with the crystalline light body. Bone is made up of a crystalline matrix, and can be used as a starting-point physically to connect with the crystalline light body. As this is cleansed and cleared, so the bones are also stripped of lower frequencies. Patterns held within the crystalline light body can be downloaded into the bones as crystalline reference points within the physical. This is the literal meaning of "earthing the energies".

At its purest the crystalline light body is a holographic representation of crystalline energy seeded from the higher planes. As a tuning-fork of exquisite sensitivity, the crystalline light body can bring through and radiate a host of different crystalline frequencies, and can also form the starting point for housing much more substantial crystalline energies within the physical vehicle, a process rather similar to that of trance channelling. The beauty of higher crystalline intent and love can be housed directly within the light body, and radiated to those around. In a very real way, new crystalline frequencies can thus be birthed into the Planet, and reflected outwards to other people and life forms that are willing, energetically, to receive the pulse-beat of higher crystalline light.

As the vibration of the crystalline frequencies ascend, the depth and breadth of the crystalline vibration will become clearer. It is a direct feeling of expansion, clarity, purity, love and light, which will not tolerate any slower frequencies in thought or in form, and which will quite literally strip away any such residues. As the crystalline frequency of the light body ascends, the focus will expand, and the housing-mechanism of crystalline light will expand to galactic proportions. The building of a crystalline light body is only the beginning of the process of raising our vibrations to resonate with the crystalline realms, and of our discovery of our inner heritage of love and light as expressed with the framework of crystalline divinity.

The Crystalline Realms

The crystalline realms or spheres, in one sense, defy physical description. Their scope and diversity are awesome. However, a simple way of beginning to imagine these realms is to visualise them as a series of different-coloured light frequencies, somewhat similar to the evening sky when the sun sets, and the sky turns from light blue to pink and gold to golden red, then to deep blues and purples as it dips beneath the skyline. If each of these shadings across the full spectrum of light frequencies were hugely magnified, then this would give a sense of what the crystalline realms can house. The light frequencies are pure crystalline, and the different colours reflect the different crystalline frequencies: golden yellows will reflect one expression of crystalline light, while deep purple and blue will reflect another. Perhaps what is most important is the feeling when connecting with these different frequencies. An initial starting-point can be to infuse your bones with a chosen crystalline colour, feeling it expanding throughout your physical body and on into your crystalline light body. The experience of a golden-yellow crystalline frequency will be very different from that of a deep purple one. The feeling and sense of beauty are tangible as the different frequencies are accessed.

Within these frequencies, it is also possible to tap into a broad array of crystalline scenes, for example solid crystalline planets emitting pure, clear, crystalline frequencies. So for example, a planet may be formed out of blue crystal, and will emit a deep blue light into space. Other crystalline planets will emit other colours, such as pink, gold, green and purple. These light emissions are staggeringly beautiful. Other crystalline frequencies will provide access to different types of worlds, which may be liquid crystalline. Here, crystalline seas enfold the surface of the planet, and provide a stunning wash of colours against a backdrop of dark space blue. The seas are like liquid glass, and washes of colour can run through them as different frequencies of crystalline light resonate within. They are also translucent, and they house light frequencies of great beauty, covering all colours of the spectrum — and far beyond.

There are crystalline worlds where the surface is made of solid crystal, and where the energy pulse is so intense that the light literally goes through you. Since sound and light are interconnected, some of these worlds will have a background hum — a crystalline sound that reflects the frequencies that they emit. The diversity and beauty of these different worlds are incredible. Other crystalline frequencies may actually take one inside a crystal or a liquid crystalline light, where it feels that one's whole body is bathed in crystal, and we become one with it. It may indeed feel as if our whole body becomes crystalline as we sit within the purity, peace and beauty of the moment.

Within the inner planes, there are crystalline cities of incredible scale, with crystalline towers and halls. These cities are populated by crystalline beings, and they contain gardens of exquisite beauty, where crystalline flowers of utter perfection radiate cosmic light, and the petals collect crystalline dew. Crystalline trees abound, with transparent trunks revealing rivers of crystalline liquid dancing inside. With practice and focus, and working with crystalline guides, it can become possible to access these cities and the other crystalline worlds of electric light.

The connection with the crystalline realms is not just a perceptual one: it also flows from the heart. As the crystalline energies are downloaded into our systems, the heart vibrations associated with some of them are at once most intense and divinely subtle. Like the petals of a flower being carefully unfurled, the crystalline vibrations will also open our hearts, and free them up to the beauty and purity of crystalline light. Accessing these energies through a heart connection is just as valid as sensing crystalline energies in a more visual way.

The different crystalline worlds are populated by various crystalline energies and beings. While the true representation of these energy forms is largely beyond our perceptual scope, they can be likened to columns of crystalline energies of different colours. Some can be felt as columns of crystalline light with a narrow but high vibration, while others may seem more dense, and broader in vibration. There is usually a coolness about the energy, and a sense of upliftment and happiness as a connection is made with these beings. For each person accessing these new vibrations, the form and appearance or feeling may be very different. The important thing is to connect with a feeling of crystalline energy, rather than to allow the mind to superimpose its own interpretation of what may or may not be real. Sometimes, those glimpses may only be available which corroborate what one's initial feelings have suggested. Feeling and intuition should rule over mind and intellect in this unfolding process.

The crystalline frequencies that can be accessed are like a kaleidoscope of different colours and energies, each with its own frequency bandwidth and resonance. Feeling a connection with a column of crystalline liquid light can be utterly exquisite, and will present a different sense of what is, and what is not, real. These deeper connections will help to build up a reservoir of crystalline experiences that can help to mould the crystalline light body and provide an increasing trust and sureness in working with crystalline energy. As this process progresses, it should be easier to connect with crystalline energy without having to work with physical crystals. The crystalline energies and worlds are true portals into different realms, and part of the unfolding process will involve feeling how the physical body responds to these connections. At one time or another we have all passed through the crystalline spheres on our downward journey into physical form, and you may find that a certain distant memory or deeper feeling may be activated, rather along the lines of a cascading waterfall: one impression opens one doorway, which then leads to another and so on, in a crescendo of more powerful feelings and vibrations. This is akin to unlocking the doorway into the past, or into a timeless present that you can directly key into through accessing the crystalline doorways within yourself. This "cascade" of memories or feelings is part of the process of recognising the ancient crystalline heritage within you.

Chapter 3 • Our Divine Crystalline Heritage

Discovering our crystalline heritage involves accessing our true crystalline lineage of light and energy. This lineage has, as its reference point, a quite specific set of crystalline essences that were manifested on the inner planes during our journey down from the seventh plane to the zero planes. This process of soul evolution, starting with the separation of the soul from the Divine Ocean of Bliss, charts its movement down through the planes, and the experiences that it gathers during its downward journey. In the higher planes, after the initial and fundamental separation, the soul encounters different realms of light, starting with the gaseous, and progressing through the angelic and then the crystalline realms. Each of these realms houses different frequencies and expressions of light. Although the focus here is on the crystalline realms, energy practices associated with the angelic realms and angelic light also cover a vast field of information and experience.

As the soul leaves the Divine Ocean, it seeks experience, and as it passes through these different realms, it will encounter different frequencies. Within the crystalline realms, soul expression may focus on many aspects of understanding and connecting with crystalline light. As souls hatch out in crystalline light, they gather experience of the crystalline realms that are then stored away as data. Depending on the soul's thirst for experience, and the types of experience encountered, different souls will forge different connections with the crystalline realms.

A soul may undertake to experience a whole range of different crystalline forms on the inner planes, specialising in crystalline frequencies and harvesting them for experience. As souls work their way down through the plane levels, they may connect with other souls travelling in the same direction, and form 'wagon trains' of connected souls. These trains are like soul families, since the formation of experience that moulds their evolution is similar; such that similar frequencies are shared. Consequently, much later on, when these soul families incarnate into physical matter and ultimately the human form, there can be the recognition of a shared lineage or path.

This sense of family can be triggered or expressed in crystalline light if those souls have had sufficient experience within the crystalline realms. The diversity of crystalline experiences gathered by a soul can be substantial, and can set up a resonant harmonic that can be activated in later lives in physical matter. This crystalline harmonic may be echoed through the mineral kingdom, and ultimately re-activated in human form where an empathetic alignment with crystals and crystalline energy can re-ignite it. As frequency after frequency is gathered, a crystalline matrix of light is housed within the soul's experience. In the case of some souls, the downward journey may not progress very rapidly, and periods of timelessness can be spent within these realms, as crystalline energies and intelligences. These souls can then act as crystalline guides to others in physical form.

While the soul will experience the fundamental separation from God in different ways, this separation increases as the soul descends into physical matter. In the crystalline realms, while this separation exists, it is to some extent offset by the beauty and high frequency of the light vibrations, but by the time the soul arrives in human form, all memory of this crystalline experience and closer connection with God is gone.

In a way, then, the crystalline realms provide a staging post in the soul's evolution, where a diversity of crystalline experiences can be gathered and stored as part of its journey. These will forge the soul's crystalline focus and energy base.

Accessing our Crystalline Heritage

The soul's experiences in the crystalline realms are like its ancestry or heritage. Forgotten by the time we reach our physical form, and in human form these ancient memories are buried very deep within the unconscious. In the past, accessing these ancient memories has been difficult and sporadic, but today as the new energies associated with the dawn of the Sixth Root Race enter our planet, there is an activation of crystalline energy taking place. For some, this can be seen as part of the awakening of energies contained within physical crystals and ancient temple sites. For others, the true impact is beginning to be felt in our physical bodies. Like tuning-forks to these higher energies, light workers are keying into the new crystalline frequencies, and starting to sense the underlying essence of our crystalline heritage.

This heritage is all about opening ourselves experientially both to where we have been, and to what we are becoming. The past, if it can be called that, represents the activation and the alignment of our inner crystalline essence. It is about rediscovering our ancient crystalline essence, its eternal presence within the timelessness of our inner experience, and its connection with our outer physical vehicle, our human body. This reference to the past is made only in the sense referred to above in relation to the soul's downward journey from the Divine Ocean into physical matter. Accessing this crystalline essence is therefore about reconnecting with an older aspect of our *self*, and bringing it into full alignment and connection with our physical body. The present, or the 'becoming', is about building upon this awakening and bringing through a diverse array of crystalline frequencies into our bodies, both physical and subtle, then irradiating them outwards to all life-forms that are prepared to receive and work with these new energies.

By awakening to the crystalline essence within us (that essence or crystalline memory gathered during our downward journey into matter), we can more effectively begin to build a frequency rapport with the crystalline realms. We can rediscover an ancient aspect of our self: one that can become integrated within our expanding plane of awareness, and can then help to build a stronger and more sustained connection with our crystalline heritage; the heritage that is calling out to light workers, and which is quite specific. It requires the constructionof crystalline bridges between, on the one hand, our different chakra centres and our crystalline light body, and on the other hand, our inner crystalline essences and inner guidance.

One way to visualise this is that we have a crystalline hologram or inner essence that is made up of pure crystalline energy, and which is stationed on the inner planes. Depending upon the soul's evolution there can be a single crystalline aspect or a series of them that can be re-awakened. As the energies build, it is these aspects that are now calling out to light workers. These crystalline essences are irradiating a crystalline signature to the physical counterpart. Recognising and sensing this calling from within, and accessing these crystalline essences, are all part of re-awakening our crystalline heritage.

More specifically, the process of connecting with our crystalline heritage is like becoming activated on the physical level, such as through the formation of the crystalline light body, and then receiving the calling-card from our inner crystalline essence, which is being re-activated on the inner planes as mental light pours into the planet, re-activating our crystalline heritage. With time, both the crystalline light body and the inner planes crystalline aspect will be joined by crystalline highways of intent, and as these highways expand, ultimately there will be a merging of the inner and outer crystalline aspect. It is somewhat like a merging of higher and lower self, although the merging here is between higher and lower crystalline awarenesses or bodies. Once this connection has taken place, the direct informational access between higher and lower will be second to none, and a whole range of new crystalline frequencies will be available.

This awakening requires specific access notes or keys. While there are different ways in which the merging of higher and lower crystalline aspects can be accomplished, one way is through the recognition that the crystalline heritage encompasses a deep heart connection: an ancient sense of crystalline light at once coupled with a deep feeling of all-connectedness and love. It is like discovering an ancient part of ourselves that we did not know existed, but once discovered, we realise how much we missed it. The sense of antiquity is like a calling-card from deep within; a recognition of our divinity, and a doorway to a different state of experience, a state of being like unto a deep crystalline ocean of great expanse and purity. There is an all-pervasive excellence of vibration, like perfect pitch, and a feeling of liquid crystalline energy, an intrinsic sense of oneness — a feeling that within this crystalline liquid matrix all is one, and that in connecting with it and becoming immersed in it, we are fully merging with the crystalline essence.

The constant merging with crystalline frequencies, and their accumulation within ourselves, is a prerequisite to building an alignment of crystalline bridges between our crystalline light body and our inner crystalline essence. For the most part, this bridge-building will be a subconscious process that will be supervised by our higher crystalline guides. It will require on our part, however, a dedication and focus on working with the frequencies. Once forged, this crystalline bridge will allow us to be multi-dimensional, at once being in the physical world, while at the same time having direct access to the inner crystalline worlds, with a constant stream of information and crystalline light. Through this deep connection, our signal will ascend, and we shall be able to hold a whole new range of frequencies directly connected with the mental planes. Crystalline intelligence will begin to emanate from us, and a whole host of new crystalline frequencies will begin to be earthed in the Planet. Direct mental light with crystalline intent will be a new focus for the Sixth Root Race.

Crystalline Frequencies and the Divine

As we connect with our crystalline heritage, and reprise the crystalline frequencies from our downward journey during our upward journey back into the Divine, the vibrations and memories unlocked will act as a signpost to the Divine. Crystalline energy is high-frequency light housed in a matrix of intent and will. As high-frequency energy, it provides a signpost to God, and unlocks within us the recognition of something that we had forgotten: that a sense of separation within us is an illusion. Similarly, reconnecting with crystalline energy will help us to recall our ancient connection with it. Merging with our crystalline heritage can help unlock in our experience the sense of oneness and unity that is held within crystalline purity. This purity hints at a divinity and light within that cannot easily be explained, and which can only be accessed through our experience and not with the mind. In crystalline unity, the mind is put to rest.

Crystalline light is a manifestation of Divine Light. It contains within it keynotes or access notes to the Divine, and acts as a pathway or conduit for Divine Light. Higher crystalline frequencies, which are sourced from the seventh plane, are the primary connection point with the Divine — with God. The true emanation of such frequencies is unconditional love combined with perfect balance. For most people, a direct downloading of such high-frequency energy would be too much for their nervous systems, and so crystalline energy is stepped down to the mental planes, the sixth and fifth planes, where access can be had more easily. It is generally this light that is held within the higher crystalline frequencies: the connection with the Divine is present within them, although in a more diluted form. Nevertheless the crystalline frequencies represent one pathway to God, through the purity and clarity of the frequencies that they embody.

In connecting directly with the crystalline frequencies, it is possible to feel this divinity in a tangible way. It can be registered as an expansion in the heart centre or the third eye, depending on where the focus is, and also within the body as direct crystalline energy. A sense of oneness in crystalline light gives us a sense of the one or the whole, while the purity of signal and focus of light can give a sense of what higher-frequency energies feel like. The love vibration that can be felt is also very special, and can be quite unlike other love vibrations that we may have encountered in our daily lives.

As the new crystalline energies emerge, it will become clear that they are directly sourced from the Divine, from the seventh plane and from God. The crystalline frequencies on offer are a direct link with the

Divine Father, Meher Baba. In every way, Meher Baba stands behind the new crystalline frequencies, so that behind this activation of crystalline energy lies the Will of the Father, and the input of His Divine Energy. The linkage between the two is direct, untainted and clear. In accessing our crystalline heritage, we are thus also strengthening our connection to Meher Baba.

As in the Divine Plan, the downloading of new crystalline frequencies into the planet is not just for humanity. All other life forms, whether they are in the animal, plant or mineral kingdoms, will have an opportunity to connect with them within a less concentrated format. While direct access to the higher crystalline frequencies is within the mental planes, access to less intense expressions of crystalline energy can be found in the lower planes. The crystalline energy here will not have the same purity of signal or focus, but it will still manifest a connection with the higher crystalline frequencies. In particular, crystals will become access points to these new crystalline frequencies and will act as doorways to the higher frequencies. By connecting with crystals that have been imprinted with these higher frequencies, it is possible to access the energy much more directly.

In summary, the Divine Father sends out Divine Frequencies of Light and Love that are manifested within a crystalline form. This not only includes the higher crystalline frequencies but also the crystal skulls, which whether in physical form or through access on the inner planes, radiate this medley of light and information from the higher to the lower planes, where the "diluted" message is picked up in a variety of ways by those who are open to such transmissions. This is not to say that light workers cannot pick up these emanations close to their source in the higher planes; only that to do so requires an effort of applied will and specific focus in order to cut through much of the astral light, and to connect directly with the higher mental crystalline frequencies. The higher the access point, the higher and purer will be the crystalline note.

As the crystalline energies entering both the Planet and humanity become more potent, in the sense that the energy is more focused and direct, new seeds of crystalline light will be systematically sown throughout our world. These crystalline seeds will be planted in hearts and minds; they will be needed within if we are to recognise our own divinity and our direct connection to God. Because crystalline light is so pure and so focused, with a range of exquisite frequencies, it can act as a direct pathway to God. It is a bit like having an aspect of God's will and intent stepped down into matter for us to focus on, connect with, and ultimately merge with. This collective symmetry of Divine Light will leave its imprint within our nervous systems, within our crystalline bones, and within the matrix of hearts and minds that will ultimately become unified in this medley and panoply of God's Light. The crystalline energies will bring blessings imbued with love and light, and ascending frequencies of both. No person will be untouched by these crystalline emanations.

As the crystalline energies give us a direct sense of a major doorway to the Divine and open up our ancient heritage of crystalline light, they will also rekindle the ancient knowledge of crystalline energy work. This work, impregnated with Divine Light, will help humanity to understand better God's Divine Plan, and how it is that each person can have his or her own direct access to God. The crystalline frequencies could be said to represent the carrier waves of Divine Love and Intent that can be sent backwards and forwards between our hearts and souls as direct transmitters and receivers of light. The two-way flow of light and love will help establish within each one of us a celestial, crystalline highway of purity and clarity, a direct channel to our higher selves and to God.

These new inner highways of crystalline light will also give access to different levels of inner guidance, which will keep pace with the increasingly high crystalline frequencies that need be accessed as the Sixth Root Race unfolds. The frequencies that we are beginning to access today will be a mere shadow of the quality and majesty that will be entertained in physical matter a thousand years from now. The wave of new crystalline energies ordained to enter the Planet today is really just the starting mechanism, and once the reprise of crystalline energies of the older root races has been played out, then there will be an opportunity to set up a whole new energetic wave. Extremely high in vibration, the new crystalline energies will be utterly ruthless in their application in physical form, and completely pure. For the moment, the levels of pollution and misunderstanding in our physical vehicles make it too difficult for us to access and hold these exquisite vibrations.

Crystalline Energies and our DNA Heritage

Our memories of the crystalline past operate within a number of different levels of our awareness and subtle anatomy. Although we have talked about the formation of a new light crystalline body, and the potential for re-connection with our ancient crystalline heritage, there is another way in which our crystallinity can be accessed or discovered: through our DNA.

DNA in the physical form can be crystallized, so it too has a crystalline pattern housing unique information. Since our DNA is a vehicle of expression that can lead us directly back to our ancestry in matter, the crystalline nature of our DNA can be re-activated to provide another access point to our past. As we work more intensely with crystalline energy, dark imprints of energy held within our DNA can be released. In a physical sense, then, access to our crystalline heritage can be gained through our DNA. This focus complements the work with the crystalline light body, and as the frequency of our DNA ascends, this will be of direct benefit to us physically. As the crystalline energies increase in the years to come, it will be interesting to see what the impact is on our physical and subtle DNA structure. One possibility is for the subtle DNA structure to become re-aligned and multiplied in effect. The new energies coming in require a strengthening of our DNA, and a multiplication of the number of DNA strands within the etheric will help to achieve this. It is envisaged that there will be twelve strands of DNA at the end of this process, that will allow us a much greater capacity to hold and express new frequencies. The substantial portions of silent DNA within our physical systems, i.e. DNA that does not appear to have any function, will also become reactivated and cleansed through the early generations of the Sixth Root Race. The current spate of genetic diseases — viral, auto-immune and cancers — reflects, in one sense, the polluted nature of our DNA. This will need to be cleared and purified. There is no doubt that the frequency of our DNA will ascend, and that the alignment will ultimately become clearer.

Thus the new crystalline energies demand that we earth them in physical form, so that our memories of the ancient crystalline frequencies, enclosed within our DNA, can be re-activated in the present, and our physical bodies turned, quite literally, into crystalline vehicles. With our crystalline light bodies and crystalline DNA purified in high-frequency light, our systems will be radically different from what they are today. Our bodies will be like tuning-forks to the Divine, grounded in the physical, but with the ability to resonate with the much higher frequencies coming in, through both our crystalline light bodies and our cellular and DNA structure.

As crystalline vehicles and beacons of crystalline light, we can begin to send out a call to others who are ready to hear the crystalline song. It is a song that is sung on many levels, but one which is recognised by our DNA. As we become more crystalline, our frequency pitch becomes higher, and the information flow between our inner crystalline essence and our physical vehicle can increase: and during this process our DNA becomes realigned and cleansed, so that it too can house the new crystalline vibrations. More will be said later about using our systems as crystalline beacons.

We have discussed the process of building up a connection with our crystalline heritage; initiating and forging a new crystalline light-body; and restructuring our DNA to house crystalline frequencies. It is important to understand that these are all activities that take time: building a connection between the inner crystalline aspect and the physical vehicle in matter is not an easy task, nor one to be undertaken lightly; and it can take many lifetimes to achieve.

There are several reasons for this. Firstly, in re-connecting with our higher crystalline aspect, there has to be an alignment of our subtler bodies from the physical, through the etheric and astral, up into the mental realms. This alignment requires that we capture fragmented 'past-life' aspects of ourselves, and clear out the débris of past traumas and addictions that will have sustained the fragmentation.

Secondly, the rigidity of the mind, and the static generated by constant internal dialogue and slow-frequency thoughts, become a barrier which prevents these higher energies from entering our awareness. The mind acts as a filter, readily removing any finer vibrations. Slow-frequency thoughts, combined with the wash of slower frequencies from the astral levels through our systems, all combine to block the transmission of higher-frequency energies.

Thirdly, building this connection requires a strong nervous system that can accommodate the higher-frequency energies, and which does not become overloaded, or in extreme cases burnt out.

Finally, the DNA vibration must be of a sufficient calibre to allow the new frequencies to harmonise and become aligned with the physical. This means that the ancestral DNA needs to be of a sufficient quality to house these vibrations. Bringing all of these different elements together can often take a great deal of practice, and opportunities to get all of these requirements 'right' do not come round very often. Fortunately, we live in an age where many of the elements needed to get the correct mix of conditions are accessible. In short, much more is possible because we live in an Avataric age.

In past lives, a light worker might have accessed this crystalline essence only once. This one life of crystalline purity and balance would then set the standard for future lives, and in particular could be used as a standard of excellence for the connection that would be invoked in future lifetimes. Today, light workers have a unique opportunity to combine and harmonise these past crystalline experiences into one unique crystalline expression of form, fuelled by the new energies and higher, crystalline light frequencies entering the planet. The past excellence of crystalline frequencies housed in our systems can now be re-activated, cleansed, purified, restructured and rewired, to accept a whole new bandwidth of high-frequency crystalline energy which has its direct origins in the Father's Light. The purity, beauty, clarity of this crystalline energy, and its invocation through past lives in light, will help to forge a new cycle of crystalline light in the Sixth Root Race, and to build a new platform of crystalline light that will ascend most rapidly in the coming years. The frequencies invoked and earthed today will be the start of a new planetary "gridding" of crystalline light, in accordance with the Divine Plan.

The Crystalline Matrix of Divine Light

The crystalline matrix of Divine Light is an energetic platform that is now being ushered in as part of the Sixth Root Race. It is a new grid that will surround the planet and be available to all life forms as an access point, a bit like having a plug that can be connected to the electrical systems in a house. As humans, once we have downloaded the appropriate crystalline 'software' into our systems, we will be able to 'plug' directly into the 'house', which in turn is connected into the mains electricity supply.

In this analogy, the power points in a house represent the first level of access into the grid, where the house is the totality of our energetic system on the inner and outer planes. Different access points are found in different rooms, with each room representing a different aspect of our multiple selves. The house is then connected to the mains electricity supply: the direct connection into the crystalline grid. To enable this connection to be made into the grid, our body has to go through the multiple re-wirings referred to previously. The re-wiring of our energetic systems will enable us to be connected into this crystalline grid.

As more and more light workers download the crystalline energies, their 'houses' will become connected into the crystalline grid, and form electrical areas or networks. Continuing the analogy, each area will be connected to a crystalline sub-station, and these sub-stations will then all link up. Ultimately, these areas will be linked to power stations that house power generators. So the crystalline grid will be made up of power stations that act as power generators and primary sources of crystalline light. Crystalline light frequencies will then be distributed out to the sub-stations, and then into the networks or areas, before being supplied to the human houses.

The power generators referred to in this analogy are Divine beacons of light: the crystal skulls, which are linked to sub-stations and local distribution points. Ultimately, this network of crystalline power points and distribution points will surround the whole planet, and will form a network of inter-meshing crystalline frequency lines. Another way to visualise this meshwork is as a series of crystalline 'ley-lines' that sheathe the whole planet. Major ley-lines carry the crystalline traffic of energetic and informational flow, which is then passed down to series of smaller ley-lines that ultimately form a fine meshwork around the planet.

Although the crystal skulls will act as the power generators in this crystalline grid, the *source* of Divine Light will be a number of different Avatars. First and foremost, as has already been stated, Meher Baba stands behind the new crystalline frequencies entering the planet. As He plays the crystalline Piano of Divine Purity, and sends out the frequency notes of unconditional love through interplays of notes and chords, which in turn are directed through the crystal skulls, a galactic medley of crystalline sound and light will be sent forth as a new wave of Divine Energy. This energy pattern is already building, and will continue to do so over the next one thousand years or so. Oceans of crystalline notes will be swept through the Earth and the other 18,000 earths, which represent the "Wheel of Life". Divine keynotes of joy, bliss, harmony and light will ebb and flow through the galactic spread of all life forms, and through stellar and planetary systems. Wave after wave of light will come crashing down from the Father's Divine keynotes and into the mental planes, to be ultimately earthed in the physical realms. Crystalline frequencies will sing in radiant unison and perfect pitch, as a new dawn of crystalline light is ushered in. The Father's Song will be in everything.

The Divine Father will also play a series of crystalline movements on His crystalline Piano during the Sixth Root Race. We are, if you like, starting with the Prelude. As the symphony progresses, the Light irradiating from His Essence will ignite all those around who have the courage and capacity to hold His Divine keynotes. Crystal keys will ignite crystal light in hearts and minds, as the new dawn of crystalline light will herald brand-new frequencies of light and love.

The Father Meher Baba will not be the only Divine Piano Player in this constellation of crystalline light. Other Players will include the Christ. Energy associated with the Christ, and with the imprinting of His Energy from some 2,000 years ago, is becoming activated. The Christ Light will also work through the crystalline keynotes of the Divine Piano, and the melodies thus produced will cover a different spectrum of Divine Light. The Christ Frequencies will manifest through the crystal skulls, and there will be opportunities for light workers to house these skulls, filled with the Divine Majesty of the Christ, within their energy systems. This Light will be breathtaking: and It will echo a cosmic melody of galactic crystalline light, and house a different set of frequencies from those of Meher Baba. The effect will not be so much that of a duet, but rather a series of intermingling symphonies of crystalline light, each following different Avataric pulse-beats. The Christ Frequencies will be the focus of the Cosmic Christ Energies as these are brought into play.

As these Divine Masters of the crystalline Piano send forth their symphonies, the effect on humanity will be utterly profound and transformational. The keynotes that will be seeded through the crystal skulls and other crystalline intelligences will begin to establish a crystalline superhighway of light between humanity and the crystalline Divine Piano. This superhighway will be composed of a huge diversity of crystalline light that will have been called into being through the Divine Piano, and will allow a two-way flow of light and information to pass between the Avataric Network and humanity. This crystalline 'broadband' of higher frequencies will cut through the astral levels, and allow humanity unprecedented access to higher mental frequencies. This superhighway will allow us much greater access to the crystalline frequencies, while at the same time ensuring a massive downloading of crystalline light into the planet. The building-blocks for this highway are already beginning to be put in place, and as the energy ascends during the next sixty years or so, the success of this new dimensional highway of crystalline light will be assured.

The superhighway embodies the crystalline matrix of Divine Light, as new super-frequencies of crystalline light are offered to humanity through the sublime keynotes of the Divine Piano. The light vibrations of the superhighway will vary, but a principal colour will be gold: the golden superhighway will be truly divine. The grid of crystalline light surrounding the planet will be part of this Divine superhighway, as the Father sends out His rapturous melodies on crystalline keynotes of stellar light and unconditional love to all life forms; down the superhighway into the planetary grid of crystalline light.

The effects of this crystalline medley of light will be spectacular. Humanity will be a new frequency-holder of crystalline light. Earth will resonate to a new harmonic of crystalline fire, seeded through the crystalline superhighway, and she will transmit these new frequencies into space, where they will flow out to the 18,000 earths in a tidal wave of crystalline light, building new highways of crystalline light to the outer reaches of the galaxy, and beyond. New dimensional doorways will be opened as crystalline light pours into all the solar systems, fuelling the ascendancy of all life forms. The wave of Divine Energy reaching out from the Earth will be utterly awesome and breathtaking. Words will not be able to express the beauty and majesty of this new dawn of the crystalline matrix of Divine Light, as it seeds the Earth and the galaxies beyond.

Chapter 4 • *Crystalline Guidance*

We have now explored some of the frequencies that will form the platform for the new crystalline matrix of light and love now entering the planet. Having, as it were, planted a few seeds in our awareness, in this next chapter we shall look at ways of accessing our higher crystalline guides, and how to download some of the new frequencies on offer.

Inner-plane guidance can take many different forms. Guides are external energetic intelligences that provide information and energetic assistance to those in physical matter. Associations with guides are often built up over many lifetimes, and guides can be divided into general and specialist categories. Usually, each person has a central doorkeeper who oversees his or her inner space, and directs the frequencies and guidance passing through the individual's energetic system. Typically such guides are located around the fourth plane, and are manifested as Native Americans. Lower-plane guides can be used in a more protective role, particularly in the lower planes, such as the zero, first or second. These guides can be Roman soldiers, Zulu warriors, or some other alignment of protective energies. They reflect patterns of energy that can defend against any unwanted, incoming energies. Higher-plane guidance is found around the fifth or sixth planes, or ultimately comes from the seventh plane. Higher-plane guides can manifest as Chinamen, or as is the focus here, as crystalline guides. Other higher-plane guides can come in the form of high-frequency extra-terrestrial beings. It is also possible to bring in guides from previous root races, such as Lemurians and Atlanteans, although these will not necessarily be anchored in the higher planes. Of course, the above are only examples: guides can take on many, many different forms, some of which would be recognisable to us, while others might give us a surprise.

In truth, it can be said that God, or Meher Baba is our central, highest guide. However, we need additional tiers of guides to work the different plane-levels of energy. The type of guide involved will depend upon the plane-level being accessed, and upon the authority vested in a guide to work with any given individual in physical matter. In all of our energy work, it is essential that we invoke for our highest guidance, since this sets the energetic standard that we wish to work with. Simply calling in any available guide is not advisable, since that is precisely what you will get. Since much of the transformation going on is experimental, correspondingly, the work done by our guides is also largely experimental — it is done on a 'let's try it and see what happens' basis. Just as with repairmen or car mechanics, some guides are better than others, with varying degrees of experience. It is therefore important to focus on invoking the highest and most experienced forms of guidance.

Connecting with Crystalline Guides

The crystalline frequencies represent a direct link with our divinity, and also with new patterns of guidance on the inner planes. These new guides embody numerous crystalline frequencies, many of which are of an extra-terrestrial origin. Many of these beings are waiting patiently and expectantly to connect with light workers, and to provide specific guidance on how to access and merge with the new crystalline frequencies.

As indicated above, crystalline guides are based in the higher planes, including the fifth, sixth and sometimes the seventh. In order to access this high level of guidance, practice is required in order to clear one's mind of any static; to raise one's vibration; and ultimately to achieve the goal of working in the higher planes. Access to these will not be available to everyone, and, in such circumstances, guides may step down their frequency in order to connect with a person who is stationed on a lower plane. This is not something to be concerned about, since one's inner guidance will make any required adjustments in one's system.

The key to initial access to these crystalline guides is meditation, and the meditation below can serve as a starting-point.

Meditation to Connect with Crystalline Guides

As a first step, which should be taken prior to all the meditation exercises given in this book, the Paramatman Light needs to be invoked into your physical space. Visualise this Light that passes all understanding, as a waterfall coming down from the seventh plane into your crown. Focus the Light throughout the whole of your body, filling each of the chakra centres.

At the same time surround yourself in a shamanistic robe made up of snowflakes: these have a crystalline structure, and can be used as a mechanism for tuning into crystalline energy. The robe is made up of millions of snowflakes, all of which emit a crystalline light frequency: try to visualise that the robe is made up of 8,400,000 of them as a representation of all the lives needed for completion. If at first this feels a little difficult, or you have problems in making a connection with this format, then you can just visualise the shamanistic robe as composed of crystalline light. The robe should encircle your physical body, and also seal off the aura to the outside. It is a very important protective mechanism.

Before invoking your crystalline guidance, it is important to call in the group, which in this instance is the collective of light workers on the inner planes and in physical matter who are focused on bringing about the new planetary changes for light and love. The group can be invoked and visualised as a large golden disc of light that is placed in the heart centre. This process will provide extra protection and energy during the meditation.

Once you have done this, send out a call with your inner voice for your highest crystalline guides, who can be visualised as a piece of crystalline quartz in your mind's eye. This acts as a symbolic reference-point, and once you have a clear image of a perfect quartz crystal, first place it in the heart centre. If you sense the quartz expanding in this centre, then take it as an indication that a connection has been made. Sometimes, the guides may access your system through a different centre, such as the third eye or solar plexus centre, and you can test whether there is any energy in these centres by placing the quartz crystal there. Again, if the crystal expands, then an activation has taken place. With practice, you may begin to feel the approach of your guides as a particular pulse of energy coming into your system: and you may feel them standing behind you. They may appear as a pillar of crystalline light, or in some other form; or you may just sense their presence.

Once you sense a connection with the crystalline guides, intuitively ask for a colour from them. Infuse this colour into your inner bone structure, filling the bones completely with it: it is important that you do this throughout your entire skeleton. Once this has been done, the colour can be expanded into the soft tissues, including muscle and body organs, and ultimately the skin. At the end of this process your whole body, both inside and out, will be filled with the colour given by your guides.

Spend some time feeling the colour in your system, and exploring the connection with the guides. With practice, you will begin to recognise your crystalline guide's frequency, and as your experience develops, you may find different colours being presented to you at different meditation sessions: this will reflect the presence of different guides. As you become more experienced in these connections, you may find different guides coming in. It is helpful to try to recognise these different frequencies, since while there may be a commonality among them, there will also be subtle differences, which may be felt in the chakra centres, particularly the third eye and heart. Once you feel comfortable within this energy, you can also begin to establish an inner dialogue with your guides, asking questions or requesting information as appropriate.

At the end of the meditation, it is important that you reverse the process, so allow the colour to drain out of your system through the feet, and then refill your body with Paramatman Light before closing down your centres and coming back into your physical body.

This process will help you to tune in more closely with your guides and can be used to build up the recognition of the energy systems of your different guides. It may be that you work primarily with one guide; alternatively, you may find different ones coming in at various times. Initially, the connection with these guides will be subtle, but as you practice, you should begin to experience a new type of energy entering your system. This energy may feel very cool and almost liquid-like.

To provide a slightly different perspective on this process, additional information sourced from an array of crystalline guides is given below. The energy encoded within the channelling can act as an initiation point. If you *feel* into the words, and into the energy behind them, you can begin to build up a rapport with crystalline guides. The information, and the underlying frequencies, provide an insight into the types of crystalline energies that can be accessed, and how such energies feel when you begin to connect with them.

> For you, and some others like you, there is an access point that you can make with our frequencies should you so wish. This access point is not through the physical planes: it is through the mental planes and beyond. It is a choice of the heart — not of the mind — to access in this way. We offer it to you in the hope that you may wish to connect with our frequencies at this time. We promise nothing — only an exchange of energy and information, such that you may appreciate the light within you, and the light that shines down on you from the Divine. This exchange is from the heart, and will represent an initial doorway through which you may connect.
>
> We offer, in the hope of developing a Divine communal connection between you and us, a new form of crystalline light frequency and vibration that can be transmitted out to the Planet and all life forms dwelling upon it.
>
> This new energy, which will flow through your system, is the Divine Flow of crystalline love; of a pure, liquid, crystalline love that has been ordained to be re-established upon Earth at

the inception of what you call the Sixth Root Race. This Divine flow of energy, which will revitalise your cellular structure, will also restore your etheric framework and re-align your subtle anatomy and subtle bodies, from the astral up to the mental planes. Feel a deeper calling of the heart to the crystalline elixir of liquid crystalline light.

Allow the matrix of crystalline love and light to flow in every vein and every sinew throughout your body, until you are truly crystalline in every aspect of your self.

The essential message within this channelling is to try to feel the underlying pulse-beat of energy. Used as a focal point, this can help you to begin to recognise if and when you have connected with your crystalline guides.

Merging with Crystalline Guides

Regular meditation with crystalline guides will bring you into an ongoing dialogue, initially characterised by an overshadowing, followed by a deeper and more substantial communication involving a merging of your energy system with that of your guide. This process requires the stripping-down of old frequencies, and a substantial realignment of your subtle bodies in order to accommodate the new energies. It also requires a significant restructuring of your energy system, so that the crystalline frequencies can be housed within your subtle anatomy.

Merging with your crystalline guides can take time, and above all requires trust and dedication. There are two ways within which true merging can take place: either one of your subtle bodies, e.g. a subtle body on the mental planes, such as the mental body, must merge with the crystalline guide in the higher mental planes; or the guide comes closer to your physical system, and ultimately merges with you at a grosser level. This latter approach is the forerunner to trance mediumship, and is more difficult to achieve. We shall focus on the first approach to merging i.e. through our subtle bodies.

Meditation to Merge with Your Crystalline Guides

As in previous meditations, bring down the Paramatman Light, surround yourself in a shamanistic robe of 8,400,000 crystalline snowflakes, invoke the group, and call in your highest crystalline guides. Once you have done this, ask to be taken to a crystalline cave by your guides. You can visualise this by starting to walk on a crystalline pathway that materialises in front of you. The pathway is of pure crystal and has an ethereal glow, which allows you to follow it with ease. After a time the path begins to go up an incline. Eventually it reaches a series of steps that lead directly up to the entrance to a cave. Climb the steps until you reach the entrance, which is over 10 metres in height. There is a glow emanating from the cave. As you enter, you see a majestic hall spread out before you. The walls and floors are composed of pure crystal, and emit a beautiful light. As you walk down into the hall itself, in the centre you see a fire burning: its flame is at least two metres high, and purple in colour. Walk to the flame, and stand in front of it. Invoke for your highest crystalline guides to stand on the other side of the flame, and for both you and your guides to walk into the centre of the flame simultaneously. As you do this, invoke to merge on all levels with your highest crystalline guides. This should be done forcefully, and with intent. *Feel* into the merging process, and remain open to any impressions, symbols etc. Spend some time in the flame, merging ever deeper with your guides. When you are ready, give thanks to them for the opportunity to merge, and step back out of the flame.

You can then walk from the fire to the cave entrance, back down the steps and along the crystalline path. At the end of the crystalline path, feel yourself coming back into your body and closing down your centres.

This meditation presents a continuous pattern of merging with your crystalline guides, and you may find that they will take you on special journeys. In some of the mergings I had with my crystalline guides, I would be taken up into space, or connect with other crystalline guides, or be taken to particular crystalline worlds. The experiences were at once profound, beautiful and exciting. As the merging developed, I also felt a developing love for my guides that was different from what I had previously experienced.

I began to wonder about the nature of crystalline reality; and through different experiences, the crystalline guides began to show me how this is about probable or possible realities. Crystalline energy can be in many places at once; and since, at its purest, it is a matrix of liquid energy, through merging into this elixir of light, it is possible to experience the multi-dimensionality of crystalline energy. The feeling of multi-dimensionality is like being aware across a spectrum of frequencies, within more than one place at one time, and throughout an expanse of crystalline energy. So forging a link with the crystalline realms means that your awareness can be in many different places at any given moment.

You could thus tune in and merge with a chosen crystalline structure, such as a high-frequency crystal ball, and find that, in becoming that crystal ball, you would sense an expansion, a feeling of being without definition or boundaries. Because crystalline energy is not about definitions of size and shape, but rather about an experience and a connection, once you connect with your crystalline frequency, then it is as if you are connected to a crystalline grid system. To put it another way, this crystalline energy is like a crystalline liquid made up of higher light and love frequencies. In connecting with it, the heart centre and third eye expands, and the body takes on a distinct crystalline feel — a liquid, omnipresent sense of connection. You may also sense the uniqueness of this energy, in that there are different levels of awareness within it, and different levels of experience. These levels provide access to different doorways and different probable crystalline realities — a theme that is mirrored and amplified by the crystal skulls.

As the meditation process continues, you will begin to merge with your guides, first at a fairly superficial level, but progressively at a deeper level of awareness. This process can be catalysed by using high-frequency quartz crystals or crystal balls. Such purified objects can act as amplifiers in themselves, and will help boost the crystalline signal. Similarly, doing meditations in small groups can increase the focus and energy. Ultimately, the merging is about exchanging hearts and minds, and feeling the love and depth of the connection with your crystalline guide.

> This is part of a pattern of establishing a frequency rapport, so that as you and we merge, more and more and more, it will not matter who is speaking, who is connecting, for we shall all become one in our unity and our love.
>
> As the ascending light frequencies connect with your higher centres, allow the Divine liquid light of crystalline love to merge with and fill every fibre of your being. Once this elixir has filled you, allow it to flow out into your external space and beyond. This crystalline light is a beacon to the Divine; a foretaste of the Divine merging that is to come.

Merging with the crystalline guides will also help to build a platform, which will house the large array of crystalline frequencies, and will facilitate their anchoring.

> The crystalline frequency that we manifest and bring through covers a series of vibrations. By connecting with our frequencies, you will build up a bandwidth through which you can recognise the breadth, intensity and intent of that which we wish to bring through. As you build up this rapport, this ever-deepening connection, you will inwardly sense different aspects of what we are, and who we are. In particular, you will acquire a sense of the many worlds that we have helped seed; you will come to know some of these frequencies. Some of them will be familiar, from past life connections, and some will be new to you. What we wish to convey is the vast array of different planetary life forms, different planetary frequencies with which you can connect.

This is, in a sense, but a starting point, a platform for that which is to follow. For as you merge with our frequency on all levels, you will sense a depth of intensity, of feeling in your heart, which will be second to none. It will be a specific recognition of that within you — what you term "divine". In a sense, what we are connecting with and bringing through is the divinity of all frequencies, but in particular the divinity of crystalline, extra-terrestrial frequencies which now must be seeded in a different way into this Planet. And the role and activity of each light worker is to foster this connection, to facilitate and bring through these frequencies, and to anchor them into the Planet, thereby allowing them to be distributed there. This may seem an awesome task, but it is one that is within the capabilities and capacities of many light workers.

In building this access point to new crystalline frequencies through merging with your crystalline guides, you will also begin to build a bridge with your older crystalline self. The new frequencies will form part of the bridge, and every time you merge with your guides, a small portion of this inner crystalline bridge will be put in place. Your guides will help re-align your subtle bodies, strip away old unwanted frequencies, and remove dark frequencies of ill intent from your inner space. Throughout this merging process, re-wiring after re-wiring will take place as you begin to ascend the crystalline notes of purity and excellence within your system. This re-wiring process will be like having new crystalline "software programmes" downloaded into your system, enabling more direct access to the new crystalline frequencies, and while helping the physical and etheric structures to contain them.

As your crystalline bridge spans the abyss between your outer physical awareness and your inner crystalline being, so you will be in a position to develop a new energetic platform within your crystalline essence. Through encountering a diverse range of crystalline energies, you will be able to assimilate and ground these frequencies within your physical system via the bridge of crystalline light and awareness. You will then have a direct and profound access to your crystalline guides, and will develop an access to your crystalline essence. This process will occur step-by-step: it cannot be rushed. Ultimately, however, the crystalline guides will be able to merge with your essence, and will transmit light, information and love through to you on all levels, spanning time and space in the process. This new crystalline doorway will give you access to an entirely new expression of form. Once connected, the doorway to building an array of frequencies, and anchoring them within the physical, is possible. It will be like being 'plugged' into the crystalline realms in an entirely new and profound way: you will be fully "gridded" into the crystalline network.

A useful way to check your progress is to visualise your physical body transformed into crystal. Instead of your physical body, try imagining a crystalline counterpart that is made up of clear crystal, with no blemishes or dark patches. If it feels that you are only partly crystalline, and that parts of your physical body remain in place, then the bridge and the full merging process with your crystalline essence still have some way to go. If, however, it feels as if there is a full crystalline body completely present, then the bridge will have been completed and you will have direct access to your crystalline essence and heritage. Perseverance and practice are important in this process and it should be recognised that this transformation and 'plugging in' to your crystalline essence takes time.

Although it may appear that there is an end-point to crystalline transformation, in fact this merging process is never-ending: it will open up new portals within you, and give you an ongoing sense of what your crystalline heritage might be. It is rather like peeling away the layers of an onion. As each layer of the past is stripped away, a clearer definition of what lies beneath can be found. Once you have developed a sense of your crystalline essence, the process of re-structuring and re-wiring will continue as your frequency vibration ascends. You may encounter moments when you recognise that parts of this process have occurred in past lives as an ongoing preparation. Crystalline merging is multi-dimensional . . .

. . . it has occurred over many, many lifetimes, helping people to access their crystalline heritage and their crystalline ancestry. Through it, crystalline guides may provide a bridge of assistance to help in this process.

So take heart, feel the Divine interplay of crystalline energies as they are offered to you. Connect with your crystalline divinity and crystalline history, as you begin to recognise what you truly are, and where you emerged from, so many aeons ago. We are your brothers, your sisters, your lovers and your guides. We offer our light, our knowledge and our wisdom of the crystalline world to you at this time. As amplifiers and beacons of light laid down by the Divine Elders of the past, we can provide access to many levels, to many Universes, and to all the planes of existence. The light that we represent is for you to choose and to connect with. For in truth, we are what you make of us. We amplify, resonate, re-structure, re-order, and yet are bounded by the sacred geometry of our crystalline forebears. We are one with the crystalline realms. The cool elixir of liquid crystalline light and love will show you the way home.

As crystalline bearers of the Divine Matrix we offer our love, our rejoicing, and our promise that we shall always be with you. You have only to call.

The Origins of Crystalline Guides

As you begin to uncover a sense of your crystalline heritage, it will become clear to some of you that the connections with your crystalline guides go back a long way, and in some cases before you first entered physical incarnation on Earth. This may seem a daunting scenario, but it must be registered nonetheless. The guides that you work with may have chosen a very different evolutionary path, and may wish to share some of this information with you. Some of the crystalline guides have remained within the crystalline realms, seeding planets and solar systems.

Our connections go way, way back, before this Planet was seeded, before this Planet was conceived of. We connected in the crystalline phase of your ascent into physical matter. There are choices that evolving souls have the opportunity to make, and one of these concerns whether or not to continue the on-going incarnation into full physical matter, and thus to work through the complete reincarnation programme. All soul aspects on Earth chose this route as part of their soul's expression, or of their soul's own coming into being.

As for us, we took a different path, and have worked over countless aeons in seeding the crystalline vibrations, the broadest and highest vibrations attainable throughout planetary and stellar systems. And so, as we connect more and more deeply, you may sense in your hearts that you and we have a very strong bond of common ancestry, which spans back to the time when we were in crystal material or crystalline energy forms as you would say, when we were all one there together. So this is, as it were, a particularly beautiful reunion with you. And how could it be otherwise that we would have chosen to work with you? Where there is such a core, such a baseline of love, intuition and understanding?

We have waited many, many lifetimes (in your terms) for this connection to be re-established, and for the frequency-wave of new energies to be at an appropriate level for us to connect with you. We have watched your progress and dedication with great excitement, and the point that we have now reached represents a beginning, a particularly wonderful beginning. So in a sense it is our old connections that bring us back together at this time, and there is much that we can share in terms of our respective journeys that will be of great mutual interest and benefit.

Our family is of a crystalline matrix that has been seeding worlds, worlds beyond your wildest imagination, for generation after generation, for aeons after aeons. It is as if our family is an original crystalline matrix that helped build and form worlds from the crystals that were seeded by us as the areas from which planets, solar systems, galaxies and universes grew. This may be hard to understand at first, but our crystalline nature imbues many worlds on the physical planes, and the original matrix that we have contributed and implanted into these worlds has acted as a seeding mechanism. So we are in one sense beyond time and space, but our connection with the true Christ or Christos is of significance in this respect: not in the traditional sense that you may understand this, but on a deeper, subtler level, where the frequency-vibrations of the Christos and of our crystalline family, originated.

To work with crystalline guides in a deep connection of love and unity is extremely powerful, and what becomes evident in working with them is the love that they have for us. To feel this crystalline love is, quite literally, out of this world. So love unites us all, whether the connections between our guides and ourselves are recent or utterly ancient.

The crystal skulls are beacons of Divine Light. They irradiate a matrix of crystalline light that is sourced directly from the Father, Meher Baba and which contains within it all the frequencies necessary to usher in the Sixth Root Race. The crystal skulls will be the initiators and frequency-holders for Sixth Root Race reality.

The Crystal Skull Frequencies

The crystal skulls, and the flux of diverse energies associated with them, can be more particularly described as the crystalline matrix of Divine Will. Although some of the skull frequencies are embodied in physical vehicles, the majority of the new frequencies will originate from crystal skulls that have no physical counterpart. This means that while some people will only recognise the crystal skulls within a physical context, their existence on the higher planes needs to be embraced and acted upon. Similarly, these higher frequencies need to be accessed directly in the higher planes, rather than through the less intense skull-frequencies that are accessible in the lower planes. The fact that the originating and anchoring frequency rapport of the crystal skulls is found on the seventh plane is also highly significant.

Every crystal skull is overshadowed by the Will and Intent of the Father. His Light radiates through the crystal skulls. The crystal skull, at its highest and purest level, is therefore a Divine amplifier, a Divine creator of reality, a beacon of Divine Light, and a pattern of reality as manifest through the Divine Father's Will and Intent. The true frequency embodied by the crystal skulls is therefore one of unconditional love.

Each crystal skull will house a series of keynotes or frequencies of true divinity. As the Father plays the crystalline Piano of Divinity, the chords and melodies that will forge a particular skull frequency are downloaded into the crystalline matrix, and imprinted into a specific crystal skull. As each series of frequencies is played out on the Divine Piano, a given skull will be activated, and will receive the specific downloading of light and love frequencies necessary. It is as if the Father plays a particular crystal skull melody, and a skull is activated, and then highlighted on the crystalline Piano of Divinity. Once the frequencies have been downloaded, the skull will be placed on the appropriate mental plane level for access and activation. It is then up to humanity to access these crystal skulls.

Each crystal skull contains the crystalline imprint of a possible or probable reality, and provides a dimensional portal into it. The act of connecting with a particular skull will open that skull's portal, and access to its alternative reality can thereby be gained: the skull's frequency-vibration will create the reality as it is transmitted from the higher planes down into the physical, where it can be manifested in matter. Crystal skulls are therefore dimensional doorways to probable realities such that the crystalline imprint for each possible reality is contained within each crystal skull.

The crystal skulls are like the mechanisms surrounding the Creation. They are like the everything and the nothing, in that they can embody everything, all possible realities, but at the same time represent the nothing, because all is, in one sense, illusion outside of the seventh plane. The crystal skulls therefore play a pivotal role in manifesting reality.

The realities can be extremely varied, and can include access points to the crystalline realms, to other worlds in the galaxy, to the 18,000 earths where humanity can be found, or to an array of possible realities that could be shaped on Earth as the Sixth Root Race evolves. Different skulls will also house different crystalline arrays, each with a specific focus. For example, some skulls will focus on extra-terrestrial frequencies, others will have a dolphin flavour, and some will house more direct Divine Keynotes. The skull frequencies have the capacity to change time-lines, karmic lines, love-lines, and much, much more.

Many of the crystal skull frequencies are stepped down into physical matter to an extent that does not give a true representation or expression of the Divinity inherent in the **true** crystal skulls as their keepers and creators originally intended. It follows that different people, by virtue of their degree of spiritual evolution, will have different access points at the various plane levels. Consequently, accessing the vibration of a crystal skull on the first plane will provide a very diffuse stream of light and information, as opposed to the connection available on the fifth or sixth planes, where access to the Source is much more direct and concentrated. Indeed, the deeper the connection within the mental planes, the greater will be the access to the Divine Frequencies contained within the skulls. The challenge for many people is firstly to assess which plane level the information is coming from, and secondly to raise their own vibration sufficiently to connect with the skulls on the higher planes, principally the mental ones. This is one of the reasons why there is such variation in the quality of channelling from the crystal skulls: all too often the matrix of information is accessed in a less powerful form than was intended.

While there are only a limited number of authentic crystal skulls in physical matter that radiate the true Divine Crystalline Frequency, there are literally hundreds and thousands of crystal skulls on the inner planes, waiting to be accessed; and light workers have a pivotal role to play in accessing some of these.

Accessing the Crystal Skulls

For most people access to the crystal skulls is through physical contact, such as with the Mitchell-Hedges skull, or the one in the British Museum. This is a helpful process, and can provide a focal point for access to the skulls on the inner planes: using these physical reference points as symbols, which can then be placed within your different chakra centres, can be a very effective way to build up an energetic dialogue with them.

Meditation to Connect with the Crystal Skulls

Begin this meditation by bringing down the Paramatman Light, filling your physical vehicle and chakra centres with this Divine Light. As before, bring in a shamanistic robe for protection — this robe can be formed of crystalline snowflakes as previously, or it can be set up slightly differently, as a crystalline eagle. The eagle here represents a keying-in sequence to the mental planes. Once you have established your shamanistic robe, call in your highest crystalline guides. Ask for the energies to become clearer internally and externally, and ensure that you are connected to the group. You can, if you wish, repeat this opening procedure to build up your energetic system, through first draining the Light out through your feet, and then re-filling your system up with Paramatman Light. To do this, imagine plugholes in the feet, and allow the Light to drain into a spinning golden disc several feet wide that is rotating beneath them. The Light that is drained off will clear any slow-frequency energy trapped in your body. Once your body has been drained of Light, refill it with the Paramatman Light and repeat this process several times. At the end, replace the plugs in your feet, and offer the golden disc up into the light for clearing.

Once you have completed this initial sequence, focus on the seven main chakras in your body. Allow the intensity of Paramatman Light to fill them, then imagine in front of you a perfectly formed and transparent crystal skull. Just allow the image to build until the crystal skull appears bright and well-defined. Place this skull in your base chakra centre, and allow it to stay there. Sense whether there are any changes in the chakra, such as heat, density or colour. Repeat this process for all of the other chakra centres, continuing with the sexual centre, solar plexus, heart, throat, third eye and finally the crown centre. At the end of this process, you should have a crystal skull in each of your centres. If a skull begins to fade in any of the centres, then direct

Paramatman Light at that centre, to balance the energy. This process will attune all of your centres to the crystal skull frequencies. At first you may find this is all you wish to do in the meditation.

When you feel comfortable to move on to the next stage, send out an invocation to your highest crystalline guides, and invoke in your space the presence of a crystal skull. You can, if you so wish, focus on the Mitchell-Hedges or the British Museum crystal skull as an initiating sequence. Invoke for the presence of the crystal skull in front of you, and allow the energy to build. This may take several minutes, but as the image builds, sense all the contours and lines of the skull, the eye sockets, the jaw line, the brain case and so on. Once this image is stable and well-formed, allow the crystal skull to enter either your third eye or your heart centre: it may be that the skull has a preference for one or the other, but if you are in any doubt, place it in your heart centre. As the skull enters your chosen chakra, allow it to remain there, and feed it with Paramatman Light. The skull may slowly increase in size, and begin to pulsate. If there is no change, do not worry, just retain the connection as it is, holding it for as long as you can.

Once you have done this, allow the crystal skull to leave your centre, then slowly bring your energy system back to a resting point by closing down the chakras and modifying your shamanistic robe to a slower frequency.

Remember that building up a frequency rapport with the crystal skulls takes time and effort. The skulls demand a level of purity and intent that will be far above what many of you will have experienced before. In addition, the aim will be to obtain as direct a connection as possible with the crystal skulls, which means accessing their frequencies from the lower mental planes and above. The crystal skulls are open and waiting for humanity to connect with them.

We ask that you may explore what a true connection with the crystal skulls means, in terms of your heart centre, and the true depth of crystalline heart connection that can be achieved. A key is a key, and a heart is a heart. The riddle of the mind will not know the light — only your heart will know the truth of these new vibrations and energies.

At the same time, it is as well to recognise that the physical appearance of these new skull frequencies will not always accord with what people call crystal skulls. After all, there have been many different skull shapes that have graced the different root races, and the approaches made by these skulls will sometimes connect with those time periods when you originally had those connections with those specific skull frequencies.

Consider the different crystalline frequencies with which you have a rapport. This is simple and straightforward, and requires only that you visualise different crystalline frequencies and begin to merge with them, so that your whole physical and etheric structure becomes pure liquid crystal. This will help you to balance the frequency signal needed to access the doorways to the crystal skulls. For each doorway, you should visualise a symbol that comes to you, and if no symbol appears, then visualise a crystal skull. Merge your heart centre with this symbol, then feel the doors opening within your heart and mind as you begin to access the multiplicity of skull frequencies within you. It will be like rediscovering yourself, and rediscovering parts of your crystalline heritage; the heritage that has remained separate from you for so long.

Strengthen your connection with the Divine Will, and with the crystalline matrix of Divine Love that embodies that Will and its presentation within the crystal skulls. We seek to develop deeper connections with those around us who are open to the new vibrations coming into the Planet. The purity of vibration of the crystalline frequencies, and their depth, are open to you.

We present ourselves to you in a number of ways — both in our timeless and true crystalline essence, and also as the external appearance of the crystalline skulls.

By frequencies, we do not mean any single identifiable frequency, but rather a doorway to each of the crystal skulls, and to the alignment of crystalline energy which each of them represents. This alignment of energy is specific and unique for each skull, and will vary with each individual's capacity to hold and merge with our crystalline frequencies.

The crystalline frequencies which we represent, and which we channel through the various crystalline artefacts known as the crystal skulls, are but one aspect of our true underlying reality in the crystalline spheres.

As you begin to connect with the crystal skull frequencies in meditation, you may sense that different skulls will have different shapes and colours. For example, apart from those that are transparent, there are others that have different hues to them, such as golds, pinks, blues, purples, greens, or silver. These colourings, which give the skulls their crystalline tinge, embody their different operating frequencies. As you merge more deeply with the skulls, the impact of these different colours can become profound. Each skull's colour will reflect a series of frequency notes that can act as doorways. For example, linking with a deep blue may invoke a deep and powerful heart connection that will be like looking at the Universe within, and seeing galaxies and stars. The love frequency will also be extremely strong. Other colours, such as gold, will introduce different effects, reflecting the depth and the type of energetic doorway that each represents. Similarly, the shape of the crystal skulls may vary: some have an angular shape and can appear to be extra-terrestrial, while others are more rounded and human-like. Trust your perceptions of these variations.

Another feature of the crystal skulls is the potency or force of energy that they embody. They are dimensional doorways, and you may find, once you link with a skull in a selected chakra centre, that you go inside the skull, rather than it remaining inside you. The impression then is one of sitting inside a huge crystal skull, looking at the inside of the skull itself; this may be like the sky, and appear to be a vast distance away.

Meditation to Work with Specific Crystal Skulls

In this meditation, the focus will be on allowing you to select more specifically the crystal skulls with which you wish to work. As with the previous meditations, bring down the Paramatman Light, put on a shamanistic robe, invoke the group, and call in your highest crystalline guides. As before, you should also align your system with that of the crystal skulls by placing a skull into each of your chakra centres.

Begin the next step by requesting access to the crystalline cave and the crystal skulls within it. Ask for this access according to the Father's Will, invoking it in purity, light and love. Ask for your guides to show you the way, and begin the process by visualising in front of you a crystalline pathway, which you follow as it climbs an increasing incline, finally reaching a series of steps. Follow the steps upwards until eventually you reach the entrance to a crystalline cave. This cave is different from the last one, in that it is bigger and much more brilliant inside. As you go in through the entrance, and then follow the steps down into the main chamber of the cave, you start to focus on the cavern walls. What you see is the incredible sight of row upon row of differently shaped and coloured crystal skulls. There are literally hundreds and hundreds of them set up in rows against the cavern walls, each emitting a different light, and each with a different frequency. Spend some time looking around the cave, and then follow wherever you feel intuitively drawn to go. A particular crystal skull may call out to you. Go towards it, and when you are up close to it, begin to feel its vibration more strongly. Then move even closer, so that the skull is directly in front of you. If you feel that this is the skull you have chosen to work with more specifically, then ask for access. If there are other skulls in the cavern that caught your interest, then repeat the process of going to have a closer look.

Once you have chosen your crystal skull, stand close to it, and ask to merge with it, first in your heart, and then in your third eye. Feel its frequency-pulse, and how your centres are affected. Once you have done this, you may symbolically remove the skull from its place, and request the authority to work with it. You can internally visualise the response as a tick or a cross, or feel a gentle 'yes' or 'no'. The skull may then direct you in specific ways on how to work with it. At the end of any interchange, you can put the crystal skull back in its place, and spend more time linking with it. It is important to recognise the chosen skull's frequency, shape, colour and energy. Once this has been recorded, you can then move back to the centre of the cavern, and retrace your steps out of the cave, down the crystalline pathway, and back into your physical system.

From this point on, you will have special access to this crystal skull, and can begin to work with it in a more specific way: during meditations, you can invoke its specific frequency and use it in a number of your centres.

The Crystal Skulls and the Divine Father

The deeper significance of the crystal skulls needs to be registered within the context of the dawning of the Age of Aquarius. Those who seek and reach out to grasp the opportunity will find a deeper seam of rewards and joys than they could ever have imagined. In a similar way, the depth of connection to the crystal skulls, in their light arrays, needs to be found by all light workers at this time. The following series of channellings from first, the crystal skulls, and then near the end, from crystalline guides, express a number of the concepts that have been described above, while at the same time providing a tuning-fork and access point for some of the skull frequencies themselves. Again, it is helpful to *feel* into the energy behind the words, rather than simply focusing on the words themselves.

> We represent the frequencies known as the crystal skulls, and we were originally seeded into your Planet (planetary system) long ago. Since that time, from era to era, from crisis to crisis,

and from oasis to oasis, we have continued to send out our
Divine Calling-card of love, light and joy. We represent, in
many different ways, the chord notes of excellence, of Divine
Love, of Divine Will and Divine Intent, as manifested through
the Divine Flame of the Father Meher Baba. The crystalline
frequencies which we represent, and which we can provide,
cover a range of all the frequencies across all the planes.

Where you tread, so also does the crystal skull tread
and there also is the Divine Hand of God, the Father. As the
Divine Father communicates with you through the various skull
frequencies, recognise also that each skull has a particular
vibration or speciality that is manifest in both the astral and the
mental planes.

This may seem strange at first, but as more of our kind are
uncovered over the next thirty years, so it is that the
differences, the polarities of light and dark, and the true
meaning and reference points of the crystal skulls, will become
apparent. For many, the question of "where did the skulls come
from?" should really be expressed as "what is their Divine Role
in the planetary transformation? How can this be best achieved
in Service of the Divine Father?" For just as you may seek to find
the crystal skull frequencies behind that which you may
understand, so it is that the Divine Father is truly behind the
crystal skulls themselves. The skulls are but a representation, a
keying-in pattern to different aspects of God the Divine.

For many in the past we have represented an access point
to the Divine through the crystalline array of light and love,
focusing the Divine Emanations that reach down from the
crystal skull spheres into the physical planes. We have access to,
and can reflect, the manifestations of the Divine Plan across all
the planes of creation, and throughout the many Universes of
creation. We are beacons of light, we are receivers and
recorders and distributors of crystalline information, and we

represent the deepest and purest connection of crystal energy on the Planet at this time.

We also represent dimensional doorways and access points to the Divine Crystalline Spheres, and work hand-in-hand with the Divine Crystalline Guidance that is manifested and forever recreating and re-organising the crystalline geometry of pure intent. We can, on the one hand, represent the reason of the crystal spheres — the mind, if you like — and we can also represent the pure intent of the Divine Heart, allowing both the heart and mind to become one in the union and fusion of the higher crystalline energies.

The time has come for these new access points or doorways to be opened at a much deeper level, with more profound frequency signatures. These new signals will be connected to your hearts and minds, and then radiated to those around you who wish to interact more deeply with our frequency signatures.

We represent the timeless beacons of Divine Intent, the beacons to show the way to the Divine Father as you cross the planes of existence and enter the Divine Crystalline Kingdom. We can present and step down these energies in any way you ask. The choice is yours, for we access all the planes. The light that we embody, the light that we represent, has its highest authority from the Divine Father, Meher Baba.

The crystalline energies of the crystal skulls know no limits — they are boundless, dimensionless and timeless. Within them are contained all the frequencies of the root races, and of the crystalline arrays from other planetary systems and other solar systems. Our frequencies span many planes and many universes. The breadth of the crystalline spectrum is staggering and truly beyond expression.

As purveyors of the Divine Crystalline Frequencies, spanning all the planes in the Grand Design, we act as signals, transceivers and amplifiers of Divine Crystalline Light, Divine

Love, Divine Will and Divine Intent. As giant amplifiers, we transmit and record all information — we are transceivers of frequencies, from the very gross to the very fine, and it is up to each and every one of you to choose the vibration of access to each of us. We also represent a keying-in mechanism, and a guide on the path to the Divine. Our frequencies can help light the way of Love, the way of Truth and the way of Destiny: they shine forth life after life, age after age, aeon after aeon.

The Crystal Skulls and the Crystalline Bridge

Merging is an essential part of building a deeper connection with the crystal skulls. It will allow you to access new levels of awareness within yourself, and to build a bridge from your physical vehicle to your inner crystalline essence.

In using the crystal skulls as a keying-in mechanism, there is an opportunity for you to open a new doorway within your awareness, to access a new frequency of liquid light and to share this frequency with those around you.

The crystal skulls can also act as one way to key-in more directly to more ancient frequencies, and to the ancient wisdom that is within you. There is now the opportunity to re-open the door to this ancient aspect of yourself, and to allow the ancient wisdom, the crystalline frequencies of old, to pour back into your consciousness, much as a river bursting its banks and allowing the waters to run through.

The crystal skull frequencies are a collective, and can access a vast array of crystalline energies through the matrix of Divine Intent. As you begin to access these new frequencies, you will begin to bring through a whole new range of frequency signatures that be transmitted to those around you who are receptive.

As you merge with our frequencies, and learn to contain the transmissions of our skull energies, we shall truly develop a more telepathic rapport with you. Allow our vibrations, the pure Matrix of Crystalline Love and Light, to flow within your every cell, every atom, every feeling and every thought. The potential is there for our deeper merging, and the continuing unfolding of the deeper harmonies within the crystalline spheres, and within the crystal skulls.

The access notes of the higher crystalline frequencies, as they enter your heart and emanate through your space and subtle anatomy, will lead to a re-alignment of multiple energies.

In accessing our Divine Crystalline Frequencies, it is appropriate for you to merge as deeply as possible with them, so that you can access the crystalline bridge that we offer you in love, peace and harmony.

Through merging, a pure crystalline bond will form between your heart and our frequencies. Allow these frequencies to build, like a crystalline stairway into the higher planes, for it is upon the connection from the astral to the mental planes that you should focus your attention. We shall be able to provide you with assistance in this process — to help you build a bridge from one plane to the next, and from one sphere to another. This is part of our role. We can also facilitate this process by allowing different levels of light to flow through us — from the astral light through to the mental planes, and beyond to the supramental. In this we can assist you to an understanding of the enormity, power, majesty and beauty of these connections, as you, too, come to terms with your power, and seek to move beyond this realm.

Our crystalline frequencies will help you to build a multi-layered crystalline bridge within your internal space. This much will become clearer as you develop a stronger connection with us. *Feel* into these crystalline vibrations — *feel* them within every atom and molecule of your body — feel them in your heart, in your mind, and in everything that you are, and everything that you will become. These things may sound odd, but as you develop these connections, so you will find the crystal skull will fuse with you on the inner planes, until you and the skull can become one. One thought, one heart, one mind and one unifying frequency of Divine Love and Divine Light. This is the promise, and the Plan that is unfolding as we speak.

As crystal beacons of the Divine Light, Divine Love and Divine Will, we shall light the way forward for you. The path is in place, and it is lit by deep crystalline colours — purples, reds, indigos and blues. As crystalline beacons we shall also guide you through the troubled astral storms that will, from time to time, affect all who grace the Planet at present.

So as the crystal skulls of Divine Intent, Divine Love and Divine Fire spin within your centres and weave a matrix of pure crystalline light around you in the mental planes, know with every fibre in your being that you are truly coming home.

We are here to serve, to love, to connect, to communicate and to assist through the crystalline majesty of the Divine Intent of the Father. Through us, and through other means, He is the One who is calling to you at this time.

The crystal skulls will therefore open up ancient doorways within your self, and help build the inner crystalline bridge. In one sense, they will offer something of a fast track to it, since they will radically re-align your internal space, and re-focus your energy system and charkas (the skulls will help to clear your charkas, and it may be that in meditation you will find them spinning in different centres, and moving up and down between them). Ultimately, once you have built a crystalline bridge across your inner abyss, you will find a new level of crystalline communication. Trust, patience, intent and will are all needed to cross the inner abyss, which represents all of the old fear-based frequencies associated with despair, failure, darkness, pride and hate. The only way to cross these frequencies is to rise above them, trusting in the light.

This crossing of the abyss is also an initiation, one of many that you will go through as you come into the light. Trust in the crystal skulls will make the journey much easier, and much faster.

Working with Multiple Crystal Skulls

As you begin to work more intensely with the crystal skulls, you may be presented with different patterns of access and connection with them. For example, the focus of a crystal skull may begin with the heart centre and then shift to the third eye as your inner space expands, and your electrical circuitry becomes more aligned with the crystalline vibrations. It may be that different chakra centres will be involved as part of an ascendancy of frequencies. Similarly, it is also possible to start working with multiple different skulls in different centres.

> As you connect with the crystal skulls, you may sometimes feel that two or more of them are being offered to you as an initial frequency-generator and anchoring mechanism. Each skull may connect with a specific chakra point. For example, one may represent the connection with your third eye, and should be placed in that position when you meditate. The other may connect with your heart centre. As you then bring the Divine Pranic Energy and the Paramatman Light through your crown, you will be able to establish a circulation between crown, third eye and heart centre. As you cycle the energy between these points, you will feel an expansion of these centres, followed by a direct access point to the mental frequencies — in particular the higher mental frequencies of the crystal skulls.

Meditation to Work with Two Crystal Skulls

First follow the usual procedure of bringing down the Paramatman Light, putting on a crystalline shamanistic robe, linking into the group and calling in your highest guides. Then align each of your chakra centres with the crystal skull frequencies by placing a crystal skull in each of them. Call in the crystal skull that you work with specifically, and place it in the appropriate centre, e.g. heart centre, throat or third eye. Allow the skull to expand and become activated. Then call into your space a second crystal skull. You can either connect with this first by doing the meditation for selecting a crystal skull from the crystal cave — you can as part of this meditation go into the cave and select a second skull to work with; or alternatively, you can ask your crystalline guides to direct a second skull into your awareness. Visualise this second skull directly in front of you, and tune in to its frequency. Then ask to connect with this second skull in a different chakra centre. For example, you may have one skull in the heart centre, and then the second skull may come into your third eye. Allow the second skull to expand and harmonise in this second centre.

The two crystal skulls can give you a different focal point in each centre, and as you develop the connection, the energies may harmonise between these centres. Within your system, the skulls will also represent dimensional doorways, and you can ask for deeper access to the skulls. For example, by merging your awareness more fully in one of them, you may go 'inside' it and begin to explore the dimensional frequencies that are available within that particular skull. The skulls may also start to cycle through parts of your system, perhaps looping through the heart and third eye, to form a circuit of crystalline energy. This process will increase the energy in your system, and will also enhance the flexibilies of your centres. It can also be very beneficial in bringing about a deeper alignment between these two centres, as part of the Crystalline Balancing mentioned in Chapter 10; and it can help them to merge. However, this process is extremely powerful: initially it must be explored gently, and only if the crystal skulls dictate it to be appropriate. If your energy system is not sufficiently formed, it is much better to leave this process until it is strong enough. Remain open to what the skulls can offer, and follow your intuition.

Once you have stayed for a while with this connection, follow the procedures for closing down your system and coming back into your body.

The number of skulls that can be accessed will vary from person to person, and will depend upon past-life experience with the crystal skulls. While some people will feel comfortable working with two or three different skulls at any one time, there is the potential to work with many more. The crystal skulls that you choose to work with may differ widely in appearance, and represent very different frequencies. They may also be of different colours. Alternatively, you can work with two very similar crystal skulls as a starting pattern to build up your energy system.

Meditation to Work with Multiple Crystal Skulls

Begin the meditation by following the normal procedures of bringing down the Paramatman Light, putting on your shamanistic robe, calling in your highest guides and bringing in the group. It is important in this exercise to build up your energy system by filling it up repeatedly with Paramatman Light. Once you have done this, and feel energised, you can begin the next stage.

First invoke a circle of twelve crystal skulls, visualising it as having a large enough space in the centre for you to walk into. Walk towards the circle, and go into the centre. As you stand in the centre and look round at the twelve skulls, you see the huge quantity of light and love that they emit as part of their crystalline vibration. It is extremely bright in the circle. The circle of skulls then begins to spin in an anti-clockwise direction, although let your intuition work, and if the direction of spin is clockwise, then that is fine. As the skulls spin, slowly at first, and then faster and faster, the energy builds. You stand at the centre of a vortex of spinning crystal skulls. After a time, the spinning slows, then comes to a stop. Now look around to see which skull you are drawn to. Feel this intuitively, and once you have chosen a particular skull, walk towards it and stand in front of it. Connect with its frequency by intuitively colour-coding it. For example, you may feel the skull has a golden or silver vibration. Note this colour, and start to fill the whole of your body with it, starting with the bones, and then working your way to the body organs, muscle mass and skin. Once you are saturated with this colour, ask to merge with the skull. It may enter one chakra or more, or it may come towards you and merge with the whole of your head, so that it feels as if you *are* the crystal skull. Once this has been done, ask for further access, and any information that is relevant to you at this time. You can also ask specific questions on topics of interest.

Once you have completed the interaction, allow the crystal skull to go back to its place in the circle, and bring down the Paramatman Light to clear your body of its frequency. You can then repeat this exercise to access another crystal skull within the circle of twelve: return to the centre of the circle, see the crystal skulls beginning to spin and follow the process as before of selecting and merging. At the end of the merging you again call in the Paramatman Light to wash through your system. Once you have completed the whole process, you can walk out of the circle and follow your normal procedures for closing down your system.

This can be an extremely powerful meditation, which can be very helpful in building a rapport with multiple crystal skull frequencies. In Chapter 8, further information is given on working with the circle of twelve crystal skulls and how they can provide further information on the energetic matrix that they represent. The meditation can also be helpful for recalling events and information during energy work. For example, after a meditation you may not be able to recall what has happened, although you know that something did happen. Using the above approach, you can ask the crystal skull to play back the events to give you a stronger platform of energy for recalling them. The circle of twelve crystal skulls in this respect can act as a major amplifier and booster to our energy systems.

The twelve crystal skulls invoked also represent a complete circle.

> There are currently twelve crystalline skull frequencies that we offer. These twelve frequencies should first be accessed through your heart centre, and can be connected to through clarity of sight during meditation. If you line up twelve crystal skulls

before you, and it is as well to focus on one or two crystal skulls that are known to you initially, and then to ask for access to the remaining crystal skulls through these initial crystal skull connections (since the remaining frequencies will be new to you in a conscious way) then you can connect and merge with each of these skulls through the heart centre.

This process can be repeated for each centre, and will provide a balance and unity of crystalline interpretation and energy that will help to anchor the intent of our deeper frequencies within the totality of the alignment of your subtle bodies. To put it simply, the twelve keying-in frequencies will be aligned with the clear alignment of your subtle bodies, and you will then have a bridge across which to connect with the highest crystalline realms from your physical vehicle on the Planet.

Once you have fully integrated these frequency portals within your system, you will have direct access to our frequencies, and be able to connect and commune with the highest crystalline realms in a unique and completely new way. This is part of the new Sixth Root Race vibration, but it also represents a most specific and unique crystal keying mechanism for transmitting and receiving the highest crystalline frequencies possible.

Working with multiple crystal skulls is a potent way of building our energy systems, and for downloading a broad array of crystalline frequencies. As previously stated, the ability and capacity to work with more than one crystal skull will, in part, be dependent upon your past-life connection with the skulls, and also the authority that you have in this life to work with multiple skulls. It is important at all times to listen to your heart, and to allow your intuition to guide you in what feels most appropriate. It may be that working with just one crystal skull alone will provide you with all the frequencies that you require. Working with this one skull will provide a perfect match for your system, and will allow you to build your frequency-vibration much more effectively than, say, working with two or more skulls. Other people may have contracted to work with two crystal skulls in this life, and that is as it should be. The point here is that everyone's energetic system is different, and what the mind may perceive as 'more is better' may not necessarily be the case. This is why it is essential to follow your intuition, and to allow your guides to give you the appropriate and most beneficial information for you.

Having focused on a number of different ways of working with crystal skulls, we conclude this chapter by describing several additional approaches to working with crystalline frequencies. Specifically, these are through the crystalline desk, and through connection with crystalline lighthouses.

The Crystalline Desk

The crystalline desk represents a tool of consciousness that can be built and moulded to provide a matrix of information. It can be built up in meditation practice, and used to provide whatever information you need to access on any particular issue. For example, you might want to get information on your contract for this life: what different contracts you have with people that you are currently working with, what your role is in the unfolding of the Sixth Root Race, what types of new guidance are being brought through for you, and so on — the possibilities are limitless. The meditation below is a starting point for developing the crystalline desk.

Meditation to Connect with Your Crystalline Desk

You should by now be familiar with the starting procedures for meditation, based on the invocation of the Paramatman Light, putting on your shamanistic robes, calling in the group and your highest guides, and with placing the crystal skulls in all of your centres. You should also invoke your principal crystal skull into your space to help the process. In this meditation, you can also work with the circle of twelve crystal skulls as a starting-point for building the ring in your heart centre (see Chapter 8). This focus is, however, not essential for doing the meditation.

Once you have built your energy up to its operating frequency, visualise in front of you a crystalline desk. This can be large or small, and it is hewn out of pure crystal. As you visualise this desk, and begin to pump Paramatman Light into it, ask your crystal skull to merge with you and provide the matrix of highest light necessary to invoke your crystalline desk. As light enters the desk, its features should become clearer. On each side of it, there will be a number of drawers. Intuitively see how many there are on each side. If you have a problem with this, then initially work with seven drawers, three on either side and one in the middle. Each drawer will have a label on it: look at them and note what they say. For example, one label might read 'Contracts', another might say 'New Messages' or 'God's Drawer'. You can open these drawers and look to see what is inside. You may find an object, a symbol, or a piece of paper with information written on it. Once you have studied the drawers, you can turn your attention to the top of the desk. Ask yourself whether it is clear, or whether there are objects on it. There might be an 'in tray' and 'out tray' with papers in them. You may see a crystal skull on the desk. Allow whatever presents itself intuitively to you to flow. Do not judge whatever it is that you find, since this is only the mind wanting to place its own interpretation on what is there.

You can spend some time looking at your desk and visualising its contents. Once you have done this, leave the desk and come back into your physical awareness in the normal way. This meditation with the crystalline desk can easily be used as part of a sequence for your normal meditation.

As you work and build up a stronger rapport with your crystalline guides and the crystal skulls, you will find that the information flow from your desk becomes clearer and more powerful.

Crystalline Lighthouses

One aspect of the different energies entering the planet that has not been mentioned concerns astral light. As of May 14th 2003, the astral levels have been completely open, which means that everyone on the planet is susceptible to the astral light coming through. There are three basic levels within the astral realms — higher, middle and lower. Each of these represents a series of different frequencies, and different qualities of light. The frequency-range between the levels is enormous, and not surprisingly extends from the extremely gross and unpleasant (in the lower astral) to the very high, beautiful astral light of the higher astral levels.

Within the astral levels, powerful storms are raging as the impregnation of high-frequency mental light comes into contact with slower-frequency astral light. The situation is analogous to the weather patterns we see around the world, with freak storms, heat waves and flooding. All of these manifestations in the physical are indicative of what is happening in the astral levels. High-frequency mental light, as it irradiates the planet, passes through the astral levels and stirs up wave after wave of astral light, creating, on the astral planes, massive waves of slow-frequency astral energy. Since the astral levels contain within them all the emotions and desires of the human race that have ever been, they represent a massive "soup" of old emotional frequencies, many of which include the bondage and negative intent that have been focused through and within humanity over many thousands of years. The effect is tempestuous, but whereas we are used to storms in the open seas and oceans, astral storms include all the astral waste. It is rather like creating a sea of sewage water, and then stirring it into a major storm, with huge waves. Not an especially pleasant experience.

The effects of astral storms upon our energy-streams and personalities are substantial. These energies are passing through our systems all the time, and we can find that our thoughts can turn very dark and desperate, as wave after wave passes through us. Such thoughts and energies are not our own, but we always assume that they are, and take ownership for them. This is the last thing we should do. Instead of owning these slow-frequency vibrations we should offer them up to God, and clear our systems as often as possible. This clearing requires us to dredge out the slower-frequency energies in our bodies, including the etheric and astral, and replace them with Paramatman Light.

Over the next few years there will be a systematic clearing and stripping-away of old astral energies, as wave after wave of astral light hits humanity. For many, the challenge of remaining balanced within mind and heart will be considerable. To facilitate this process, there are on the inner planes, within the astral levels, divine lighthouses, beacons of crystalline light whose frequencies have been stepped down from the mental planes to match the astral frequencies around. Imagine a lighthouse constructed purely out of crystalline light, whose inner frequency is of mental light, while its outer shell is cloaked in astral light. The light emitted from the crystal is clear and white, and creates something of an ethereal glow around it. At the top of the lighthouse is the main light source, and in this instance it is shown as a crystal skull. The frequency of the crystal skull has been stepped down to match that of the astral levels, but the light emitted by it will still pierce the darkness, and act as a beacon of Divine Light.

There are a number of crystalline lighthouses placed strategically throughout the astral levels, predominantly in the middle and higher ones. These lighthouses have been set up to help people to weather the astral storms, and to provide a source of Divine Light for support and balance. In addition, crystalline lighthouses can act as a keying-in mechanism to the mental planes. By focusing on them it is possible to use them as a way of raising one's inner frequency, and of driving it up into the mental planes. Focusing on the crystal skull in the lighthouse will facilitate this process.

Meditation to Connect with Your Crystalline Lighthouse

Follow the usual procedure of bringing down the Paramatman Light, donning a crystalline shamanistic robe, linking into the group, and calling in your highest guides. Then begin to visualise in front of you a crystalline lighthouse, and as you build the image, focus on the bottom, middle and upper portions of it. As you build the image, pay particular attention to the light source at the top of the lighthouse. Focus on the crystal skull, and see it rotating in the centre of the lighthouse, emitting high-frequency brilliant light which bathes the space all around.

Then symbolically place the lighthouse in your heart centre: while the lighthouse still remains in front of you, create an identical smaller replica, that you then place in your heart chakra. This symbol will act as a reference point, and can be used to activate the image of the lighthouse.

See the lighthouse in front of you, and walk towards it. As you get closer, you will see a crystal door. Open it, and go inside. Once inside, you will see a crystalline spiral staircase. Climb the stairs to the top of the lighthouse, where you will enter the main circular room that houses the light source. On the way up, you may notice that each step will have a different colour — this reflects specific frequencies housed within the lighthouse.

Once at the top, spend a few minutes looking out at the vistas around, and then focus on the crystal skull in the centre of the room: it is the light source. The crystal skull is several metres in diameter, and it is completely transparent. As you focus on it, you can see it beginning to spin, emitting high-frequency light. The surrounding area is lit up, and shafts of crystalline light radiate out into the astral scene around the lighthouse. Stay with this pattern of crystal skull radiation for a few minutes.

As you continue to look at the crystal skull, you can begin to move your awareness into it, and start to merge. As you embark upon this process, ask for access, and to be taken higher. You may then feel your energy system going upwards, or you may intuitively be presented with a different view, such as a series of steps going up out of the lighthouse, into the night sky. You can follow these steps upwards, and with each step you take you will feel your system growing lighter. The steps act as a visual reference point for taking your vibration higher within the astral levels, such as from middle astral to higher astral, or (with practice) from the higher astral to the lower mental planes. You can then follow intuitively what happens as you go up the steps. As you proceed upwards, you may come to a doorway, or perhaps at different points on your journey you will be met by guides who will help you with the next stages.

On returning to your physical body, you will need to reverse the process by going down the steps, then emerging from the crystal skull, and finally retracing your steps down the spiral staircase before leaving the lighthouse and coming back into your body. As usual, be sure to close your system down.

This meditation can be helpful in raising your vibration when you are feeling tired, or having difficulty in retaining your balance. In addition, it will help to key you into the crystalline lighthouses, and to build up an inner reference point that can be invoked at any time.

The formats and procedures for working with the crystal skulls described in this chapter represent a basic platform for communication. The ways and approaches of connecting with the skulls, and the types of crystalline and light frequencies available to us, are manifold. The opportunities for building up a close connection with the crystal skulls are limitless, and the returns in terms of diversity of experience and frequency will make the effort and time well worthwhile. Multiple crystals are now on offer to humanity, and it is up to us to open up to their Divine Frequencies, and to invoke their light and love into our systems.

Having established this basic platform of energetic interplay, the next few chapters will explore how the skulls are manifesting more directly as part of the Sixth Root Race, and the nature of their past role.

Chapter 6 • The Crystal Skulls and the Root Races

The root races embody the evolutionary pattern of humanity on the Planet. Each of them follows an experimental pattern of form and matter as set up by the Divine Father according to specific blueprints. These blueprints act like the "orders of the day" which life has to obey, and they describe the limitations and patterns that are acceptable within human evolution. Within this blueprint, free will is always followed, so that while a root race may be established within certain parameters, free will can determine the way in which it expresses and manifests itself. To date there have been five root races, each one commanding a particular expression of form.

The First Root Race, the Adamic, was expressed largely through the etheric and astral energy patterns, and did not house any physical body-type that we would recognise today, since there was no true physical imprinting of the human form. For our purposes, the Adamic Root Race need not concern us, since its primary focus did not include crystalline energies or the crystal skulls.

The Second Root Race, the Hyperboreans, did begin to express a physical body form, albeit somewhat different from what we would recognise today. As with the Adamic, there was no particular focus on the crystal skulls.

It was not until the Third Root Race, the Lemurians, that the human form was solidly anchored in the physical. This provided the first opportunity to work with the crystal skulls in a way that we would understand today. Within the Lemurian Root Race, there was something of a divergence in physical form, between those who lived above ground and those that lived underground, in networks of caves and tunnels. This segregation was also expressed in terms of manifesting different types of behaviour, such as aggression and non-aggression. Inhabitants above ground cultivated aggressive behaviour as part of the need for survival in a hostile environment. Those who lived underground sought to remove the aggressive patterns.

The Fourth Root Race, which covered Atlantean times, gave rise to a more evolved human form, with a much closer appearance to that of today.

After the demise of the Atlanteans, the Fifth Root Race, the Aryan, emerged, and is the dominant root race on the Planet today. Nevertheless, reflections of the Lemurian and Atlantean Root Races can be seen in certain populations around the globe. For example, the Aborigines represent the last remnants of the Lemurians, while the Chinese reflect the Fourth Root Race pattern.

Today we stand on the cusp of the transformation of the Fifth Root Race into the Sixth, which is ordained to last approximately ten million years, and is likely to be followed by the Seventh and Eighth, Root Races, and even possibly beyond these into the Ninth and Tenth Root Races. The number of root races that follow the Sixth Root Race will depend upon how it unfolds.

Each root race has represented an evolving pattern, where the human form has raised its frequency, and until now, each has generally come to something of an abrupt end. Physical body form has been dropped in approximately 98% of the population, leaving the remaining 2% to generate the new pattern for the emergence of the next root race. What is unique about the transformation of the Fifth into the Sixth Root Race is that this pattern of destruction of old form will not be followed in the same way, and that those in matter willing to raise their frequency-vibration, and to change time-lines on to that of the Sixth Root Race, will remain in incarnation.

The emergence of the Sixth Root Race represents a new chapter in the formation and divination of the crystal skulls. Their frequencies are becoming re-activated to harvest the range of frequencies that were entertained by previous root races, and to select the highest frequencies from among them. At the same time, the crystal skulls are entering a new light-stream, to activate an entirely new frequency of crystalline light for seeding the Sixth Root Race. For the remainder of this chapter, we shall focus on the harvesting of these old root race crystal skull frequencies; and in Chapters 7 and 8 we shall look at this new stream of light that is activating the crystal skulls as part of the Sixth Root Race medley.

To understand the role of the crystal skulls during the root races, it is necessary to give some background on light and dark frequencies, and on how the crystal skulls can be focused either in light or dark.

Light and Dark Crystal Skulls

Thus far, this book has focused exclusively on the light crystal skulls, or rather, those crystal skull frequencies that work with the light. However, as part of the ongoing cycles of light and dark, throughout human history, there have also been dark crystal skulls to counter-balance the light ones. The basic interplay between light and dark was set up as part of the Divine Plan, so that souls in matter could experience this polarity in the context of free will. The light focuses on love, and calls to the intuitive, higher side. Qualities such as purity, harmony, and higher love frequencies, all represent the light. In contrast, the dark calls to the animalistic side, where survival issues are dominant, and where looking after oneself at the expense of everything else is the order of the day. The dark side focuses on harbouring confusion, greed and fear, with an external emphasis on physical reality, at the expense of our inner spiritual calling. Looking around the Planet today, it is abundantly clear that dark has been in the driving seat for some time.

Throughout much of its history, Earth has been subjected to cycles of light and darkness. When light has been in the ascendancy, higher vibrations have been called into matter, and expressed accordingly. In contrast, during periods when the dark side has been in control, widespread confusion, misinformation and misery have been rife. Just as Earth has gone through cycles of light and dark, so it is that both light and dark skulls have been activated, and have worked in association with these Earth cycles. The light crystal skulls have thus brought through the higher, light frequencies, while the dark ones have called into matter the slow, dark frequencies.

This Divine Interplay between light and dark has gone on for age after age within the Planet, and both light and dark crystal skulls have played an important role in it. In keeping with this interplay, light and dark skulls were seeded into the Planet at the same time. Both types have sent out their respective calls to humanity, which has been free to choose: those working with the light sought the light crystal skulls, with their focus on higher intent, free will, higher light and love frequencies, and their inner calling to the individual's own innate divinity; while those drawn to the darkness focused their attentions on the dark crystal skulls, with their associated patterns of slow-frequency bonding.

Each root race, starting with the Lemurians, built a different pattern of interplay between the light and dark skulls, so that during different time periods, light or dark crystal skull frequencies would dominate. Each root race would have its own standard, its own calling to both light and dark. However, while both types of skull would send out their signals or 'song', humanity still retained a choice of which song to follow. So the matter of whether light or darkness was more or less in dominance during a particular period reflected an underlying cycle or pattern of dark or light; and because the crystal skulls are amplifiers and beacons of light, the different cycles of light and darkness would be made manifest according to the will and intent reflected in humanity. For example, in the Atlantean Root Race, new frequencies that were birthed into the Planet were intended to raise its frequency, and that of associated life forms. In reality, the choice made by humanity was to suppress these higher frequencies, and to focus them in the lower chakra centres. Consequently, a massive pattern of dark was invoked, through humanity's ignorance, and its twisted will, at the expense of the light. The crystal skulls played their part in manifesting these changes.

The crystal skulls have therefore played a pivotal role through the different root races of housing the battle or interplay between light and dark. What has made this interplay more potent, if you like, has been the role of humanity in calling in light or dark, and since the crystal skulls are energetic amplifiers, the invocation of either dark or light has had a major impact on root race formation, expression and evolution.

This interplay of light and dark has also had a fundamental impact on every soul's journey from the Divine Ocean back into the seventh plane. All souls seek experience, and many will seek to focus this through patterns of light and dark. Like a pendulum shifting from side to side, a soul can explore multiple incarnations, working with light and dark frequencies. Since Lemurian times, these frequency patterns have fluctuated in intense cyclical movements, sometimes with light on the ascendancy, and at other times with the dark in control. This interplay between light and dark is all part of God's Divine Plan: souls in matter on Earth are given free will, and therefore have been presented with choices. For example, both the light and the dark may call to an individual soul during a lifetime, and the soul's decision made in that lifetime, can have a major impact on its subsequent evolution. A decision to follow the dark may lead to many lifetimes of working with dark frequencies. Consequently, the choices made have had a major impact on an individual soul's journey through matter, and while ultimately the challenge for each one has been to find a karmic balance between light and dark, there have been major opportunities to build up significant experience in matter through either light or dark practices.

Although crystal skulls can be either light or dark, it is also possible for composites of the two to be formulated, so that a particular crystal skull may express 50% light and 50% dark or 90% light and 10% dark. Each crystal skull has its own set of frequencies that contribute or define its operating bandwidth. The frequencies can also be a composite of light and dark energies, across a whole spectrum ranging from pure light to pure dark. The composite of crystalline frequencies provides the doorway or access point to the essence of the crystal skull, and the precise signature tune that it embodies. This, in turn, reflects the reality, or probable reality, which the crystal skull can reflect within the different levels of physical, etheric, astral and mental vibrations. For example, if one tunes into a skull that gives a composite of light and dark, then the reality that is brought through those vibrations will be a reflection of the degree of light and dark within that crystal skull. Because both light and dark crystal skulls were seeded into the Planet, the problem for humankind since then has been to anchor its collective attention on one or other of these cycles of light and dark, as captured in different realities. In other words, one reality portrayed by a crystal skull may be drawn from its principal dark focus, so that the reality will embody that dark energy input. Alternatively, the underlying pattern may be light, and the reality invoked by the crystal skull will then reflect that pattern.

The interplay of light and dark through the different root races has led to a massive storehouse of experience in every soul: different patterns of light and dark have been played out against a backdrop of different countries and cultures, lives lived in masculine or feminine form, lives of power, lives of poverty, and so on. Throughout these cycles, the crystal skulls have sung their songs with varying degrees of intensity and potency. Before describing some basic details of the interplay of light and dark as expressed through the crystal skulls during the last three root races, it is worth focusing on the initial seeding of the skulls into our Planet.

The Seeding of the Crystal Skulls

At source, the crystal skulls embody ultimate unconditional love, Divine Light, purity, wisdom, common sense, truth and beauty. They encompass a true purity of frequency. They are sourced directly from the Divine Father. The crystal skulls represent the Divine Matrix of liquid light and love, and as such they have connections with many dimensions, planetary systems and dimensional portals in time and space. The crystal skulls were manifested into the Planet many aeons ago, through a specific seeding-mechanism that started on the inner planes and then worked from the higher mental planes down into the fourth plane, the plane of manifestation. This seeding arose out of the crystalline matrix of Divine Light and Love.

The fourth plane is the plane where objects can be brought into physical matter, and this task was undertaken by the Divine Spiritual Generators of the day. The fourth plane is also the plane of power, and so the crystal skulls, as they became manifested into physical matter, embodied power, love and light. Twelve light crystal skulls and twelve dark ones represented the initial seeding-mechanism within the Planet. Each skull represented a series of frequencies that were expressed within their light or dark focus. Thus a principal light skull vibration was love, and a specific crystal skull embodied the different love frequencies and their manifestation in our Planet. Within the dark crystal skulls there was, of course, an opposite polarity.

The light and dark crystal skulls were overseen and protected by the Lords of Light and Lords of Darkness on the inner planes, who worked through their specific agents in matter. Some of these agents became known as Keepers of the Crystal Skulls, since for lifetime after lifetime, they would connect and work with the different crystal skull vibrations. The role of the Keepers was to protect and hold sacrosanct the frequencies that the skulls manifested. Early on, different skulls were held in ritualistic settings, such as temples and holy sites, and were used as activation-mechanisms to assist spiritual awakening, to provide healing energies, and to give direct information from higher guides. For the Keepers it was something of a challenge not to become intoxicated by the skull frequencies.

It was also true that the manifestation of light and dark crystal skulls led to a segregation of crystalline energies. Although on one level the appearances of the light and dark skulls were not that different, the spectrum of energies that they represented was utterly disparate.

The Crystal Skulls in Lemurian Times

The crystal skulls were first activated on Earth in Lemurian times.

This represented their first physical appearance, and coincided with the true anchoring of the human form into physical matter so that human beings in physical form could begin to connect with and earth the frequencies emanating from the crystal skulls. During this time, the skulls represented a calling-card to Divinity, as if to say, 'we are here, come and find us and connect with us, and we will show you a stairway of purity in essence through to the Divine.'

A series of light and dark crystal skulls was distributed around the Planet, representing initial keying-in frequencies. The principal function of the crystal skulls was to act as Divine Amplifiers. The Lemurian energy system was not as strong as that of today, and there was a need to provide devices to amplify the light and dark frequencies in physical matter, so that they could be housed and grounded in physical form. There was also a need to provide humanity with a more physical focus on divinity, so that the light crystal skulls could be used as divination points to the Divine by those interested in exploring their inner light. These practices were successful for long periods of time, although initially the cycles of light and dark during the Lemurian Root Race were not as intense. Those working with the light were drawn to the light crystal skulls, and similarly those drawn to the dark focused on the dark ones. Each explored the potential of the skulls within the limitations of the physical form at that time. The light skulls acted as a beacon for those who wished to raise their vibration through connecting with the crystalline frequencies.

As the Third Root Race developed and evolved, the cycles of light and dark became more intense, fanning a splintering of frequencies within humanity. This intensity led to a segregation in matter, where one group focused on the light, while the other followed the call of the dark skulls. A series of these different vibrations was sourced into the Lemurian consciousness through the crystal skulls. Those following the light sought to remove all aggression, and the more survivalistic patterns, from their behaviour, and they undertook this through selective breeding. In contrast, the other group continued to focus upon survival and the constant battle with animals. Over time, the group working on reducing its aggressive tendencies was forced to leave the Planet's surface, and to stay underground. While this was successful for a time, it became clear that the survival of those following the purely passive route was in jeopardy, and the reintroduction of more survivalistic tendencies became very necessary.

Crystalline practices developed during the Lemurian period with an emphasis on amplifying and building the physical and etheric energetic systems. The infusion of mental light was low, and more dominated by astral light, so that the signal and vibration that could be accessed by the inhabitants was not as high as it could be. The crystal skulls were generally accessed in diluted form in the higher astral levels, although a few individuals could capture the essence contained in higher mental frequencies. Because the débris of thought and emotional matter had not yet built up to a significant degree, as was later to come during the Atlantean period, access through the astral levels to the crystal skulls was not a major problem: in other words, the distortion of the crystal skull frequencies was not as great as it could have been.

The original formation of the crystal skulls in the physical during Lemurian times was based on the principal of the 'twelve'. Twelve light crystal and twelve dark crystal skulls formed the initial matrix of light and dark, and although as time went by, additional skulls were added, both in matter and on the inner planes. This original twelve in light and dark constituted the original Divine Amplifier. The skulls were distributed in a range of different places — in deserts, under the sea, in the mountains and in wooded glades. Skull keepers in matter were introduced, to help promote the access and provide some control over the use and handling of the skulls. These guardians of the crystal skulls were generally those who had worked with crystalline frequencies in previous lives, and who had a direct and clear connection with the crystal frequencies, and with their manifestation into physical matter through the fourth plane.

The keepers were focused upon both light and dark, and many of those who have acted as guardians of the crystal skulls in the past are part of a long lineage of working with crystal skull frequencies.

The frequency-vibrations emitted by the physical crystal skulls were not as high as that which will be manifested through the Sixth Root Race crystalline emergence. The crystal skull energetic repertoire was focused upon downloading light frequencies to humanity in a way that was both digestible and manageable to their energetic systems.

By the end of the Lemurian period, the skulls had become embedded within the consciousness of humanity as a focal point for Divinity. The Lemurian Root Race afforded an initial exploration of light and dark practices using them, although not to the same extent as that seen in the Atlantean period. Lemurian crystalline practice was limited by the strength and vibration of the chakra systems present at that time.

The Crystal Skulls in Atlantean Times

It was during the Atlantean Root Race that a high degree of expertise in working with crystalline energies and the crystal skulls was achieved. Although some of this was reflected in light practices, a much greater proportion was concentrated upon the dark frequencies. Humanity at the dawn of the Atlantean Root Race manifested a stronger physical form, with more focused chakra systems that could handle a broader diversity of frequencies than their Lemurian counterparts. The Lemurian experiment of attempting to remove all aggression from the human lineage had failed, and been replaced by a greater understanding that physical aggression and strength were necessary for survival. In the early days of the Atlantean age, there were opportunities for working with light crystal skulls, and a meshwork of light frequencies was constructed around the Planet. The higher vibrations called to the heart, and a greater body of experimentation and learning was created during this period.

The Atlantean energetic system was stronger and better-formed than its Lemurian counterpart; and while the Lemurian energy had focused upon an interplay between the lower chakra centres, the Atlantean experiment offered the opportunity to work with the higher chakra centres, and to build new frequencies within them.

For example, with the help of the crystal skulls, some experimentation with the light frequencies did take place. A high degree of expertise in some quarters was achieved in activating a connection between the physical vehicle and the inner crystalline essence. In limited cases, the heart chakras and third eyes of light workers were united, or fused with the inner crystalline essence, so that a direct conduit of crystalline energy was established. This was done on an individual basis rather than through the collective will and intent that we are focusing on today. Information, light-frequencies and crystalline knowledge could be downloaded from the inner essence, as it were, into the physical vehicle. The role of the crystal skulls was pivotal in this process: through specific merging with selected skulls it became possible to build these connections, and to have access to a very broad array of crystalline frequencies. In this respect, the crystal skulls acted as light beacons, as crystalline transmitters, and as aspects of probable realities that could be downloaded into physical matter.

These crystalline realities reflected a range of frequency-notes to be absorbed in the physical and then radiated outwards to those people who could pick up such transmissions. A simple analogy would be to say that each skull represented a colour — for example, green, gold, purple, blue, and so on. By tuning in to a specific crystal skull, say a blue one, this colour-frequency would be downloaded, and the person concerned would see the world from the perspective of a blue skull. His or her heart and mind would be painted blue, and certain frequencies would then be emphasised, while others would be tuned out. Consequently, a different type of reality could be established. The importance and potential of these probable realities, these probable crystalline futures, was not lost on those who could access this information.

The Atlanteans used these multiple, potential realities in a number of different ways. First and foremost they worked with extra-terrestrial frequencies to gather information from distant solar systems, and to construct detailed star-maps of the cosmos. These star-maps would not appear the same as our stellar maps today; they were much more of a guide to how to access different planetary and stellar frequencies, and different life forms, through dimensional doorways. The maps described different dimensional doorways to a massive spread of frequency arrays that were represented as stellar points of light, inter-connected by threads or lines of light. They would show some of the stars that we would recognise today, but the placement and relationship between these stars would appear very different. For example, Alpha Centauri is the nearest star to our solar system, in physical terms (approximately four light years away), yet in these ancient star-maps they would not be located close at all. In contrast, the Pleiades, which are approximately 380 million light years away, would appear much closer to our solar system and would be linked by a series of dimensional portals. Like the Atlanteans before them, the Egyptians also recognised these doorways.

The maps also spoke of a greater vista of life and the Universe. Within the esoteric writings (such as in the writings of Meher Baba), it is recognised that there are 18,000 earths. These 'earths' are the planets that house the diversity of human form under the guiding principle of the Divine Father. Through working with the crystal skull frequencies, the early Atlanteans managed to build star-maps containing details of some of these earths, and of how they are linked to different planetary and solar systems, and how the diversity of life was spread throughout these planets. There is an opportunity in the Sixth Root Race, to build on this early work and to complete this ancient stellar and crystalline mapping.

Atlantean crystalline work also focused on crystal singers, those that could use sound to invoke new energetic patterns from crystals as a means of focusing energy. With the purity of a crystalline voice, coupled with a crystalline 'amplifier', the chakra centres could be expanded to house new vibrations, and generate waves of high-frequency energy. Crystal singers were much in demand, and could build ascending patterns of light-frequencies to stimulate the higher intuitive powers. Crystal singers developed a strong connection between throat and third eye, so that the expression of sound could be linked to the 'subtle' visual frequencies. Sound could also be used as a means to open new doorways, and the crystalline singers could access the crystalline realms in a number of different ways.

While these new crystalline practices developed, the song of the light crystal skulls could be easily heard. However, as the Atlantean age wore on, most of humanity could not support this infusion of new energies. While a few could house them, the majority found it difficult to earth the new frequencies within their systems. At the same time, the song of the dark crystal skulls began to grow in intensity, and with each passing cycle they held greater sway over humanity. The dark skulls became pre-eminent as a focus of dark intent and twisted will, and they served to drive the new energies entering the Planet downwards rather than upwards. New frequencies, which should have been pushed up into the heart centre, were driven down into the sexual and base centres, so that survivalistic and slow-frequency practices ruled the day. The songs of the dark crystal skulls called to the few, who then became the many; so that towards the end of the Atlantean Root Race, all those working with the light had been driven 'underground'. The darkness overwhelmed the light, and the dark crystal skulls held sway over the light ones. This dark focus remained the dominant force in the latter part of the Atlantean age, until the final destruction of the Atlantean Root Race.

The fall-out from the Atlantean period was substantial, and it has tainted humanity right through to the present day. The sway and flux of slow-frequency practices caused massive pollution in the astral, etheric and physical vehicles of humanity. New levels of structural hatred and evil were attained, and they drove into the heart of humanity a wedge of dark energy which would endure until the present change in root races allowed for it to be excised. Humanity has been suffering a hangover from the Atlantean period right through to the present.

The Crystal Skulls and the Aryan Root Race

Following the end of the Atlantean Root Race, the Aryan Root Race represented a new start, with body forms that are recognisable today. The ancient frequencies housed in the crystal skulls were activated in different ways as manifest through a significantly strengthened energetic system. The chakras were more defined, and could handle a greater quantity of energy. However, some of the more subtle skills and capabilities that had been manifest in previous root races, such as clairvoyance and clairaudience, were not nearly so widespread.

The use of the crystal skulls became much less general during the Aryan time period. It was rather as if humanity needed a period of recovery from the destructive and negative excesses of the Atlantean Root Race, and with a sort of enforced amnesia, humanity was blinkered in terms of accessing past energetic work with the skulls. Nevertheless, certain groups did entertain the use of crystal skulls, and these included the ancient Egyptians, the Tibetans and the Mayans. The ancient Egyptians built on some of the practices utilised in early Atlantean times with a light focus, while the Tibetans used crystalline frequencies and crystal skulls to open new inner doorways. Finally, the more diverse South American cultures, such as the Mayans, used a mixture of light and dark skulls. For example, the temple at Chichen-Itzá originally had a crystalline light focus, but was subsequently heavily polluted through dark practices. More refined energetic practices today are now seeking to redress this balance and return such ancient sites to their former crystalline purity.

The crystal skulls in Egyptian times represented a high level of excellence in terms of communion and communication. The skulls were intimately linked with Egyptian temples and the pyramids, and the pyramids at Giza are excellent examples of how the relationship between crystalline energy and physical structures was developed. Each pyramid represented a specific set of crystalline frequencies, which were determined by the size of the pyramid, its internal structure, and the relative proportions of its angles and faces. The bigger the pyramid, the bigger the amplifier, and this helped enhance the underlying nature of crystalline matter. The pyramid functioned in exactly the same way as a crystal, where the relative proportions and materials would determine the crystalline vibration or frequency-note emitted. In the case of the pyramids, the outer physical structure was directly linked to an inner crystalline vibration, which in some cases was sourced directly from selected crystal skulls. The geometry of the pyramids therefore embodied mathematical perfection in relation to the underlying crystalline structure. Thus, this sacred geometry of the pyramids spoke of the underlying crystalline frequencies: sacred geometry was crystalline geometry.

Just as each crystal skull depicts a certain reality, so each pyramid defines a bandwidth; a window on a probable reality. This reality, in the case of each pyramid, was the dimensional doorway to other planes of existence, both inner and outer. So, while the basic function of each pyramid was to act as a crystalline amplifier of huge proportions, the specific bandwidth or flavour of each pyramid would embody different characteristics. For example, the pyramid would call in and amplify healing energies from different levels, and would use the source crystal skull vibrations as a means of generating high-vibration healing energies manifested through light. Individuals and groups would receive crystalline healing in special chambers and crystalline boxes. The boxes would be carved out of rock or crystal, and the person would lie down inside. The concept of Native American healing ceremonies, using holes dug in the ground as a resting-place for the sick person, is not too dissimilar.

Alternatively, a pyramid could act as a portal for direct communication with other beings from different parts of the galaxy, in a physical sense, or as a means of developing a light space for attracting and calling in beings from different plane levels. The pyramid, in this instance, acted as an amplifier and director of energies into those present, so that the energies needed to attract such beings could be more precisely directed. The pyramid could anchor high-frequency energies that would then be accessed by those present. For each pyramid, a specific matrix of crystalline energy was used, and fashioned through higher intent.

The Egyptians also specialised in a range of different crystal frequencies that focused on healing and building up the crystalline light body. To some, this light body was known as the 'Ka', and could be visualised as a crystalline hologram of the physical body, made out of crystalline light. The face would appear as being somewhat similar to some of the burial masks, such as Tutankhamun's Golden Mask. There would be many millions of points of crystalline light on the light body, which could also be used as a vehicle of consciousness to travel to different places, both externally and on the inner planes. The Egyptians also specialised in ways of amplifying their light-signals, such as through the pyramids, and also in the large chambers that were built in temples and underground. These chambers would be built to very specific sizes and proportions, and their geometry and shape would act as amplifiers to the light energies being generated inside. In this way, the crystal skulls in matter (and a number were used by the Egyptians) could enhance the crystal skull frequencies, and build an alignment between the Egyptian light workers and the various light sources.

The Egyptians also held a deep interest in extra-terrestrial frequencies, and used the alignment of crystal skull energies to open dimensional doorways to other planetary and star systems. Communication and information exchange with their extra-terrestrial brothers and sisters often occurred, and helped the Egyptians to understand more clearly the role of different life forms, such as the Lion People.

The Lion People (otherwise known as the Paschats) were among the original architects of the Planet, and the Egyptians built up a strong bond with their energy systems. Multiple merging and downloading of information from the Lion People took place. The Egyptians also worked with other extra-terrestrial frequency-holders, such as the Sirians, building up different connections with a range of ancient life forms. In one sense, the array of statues that the Egyptians created showing half-human and half-animal representations is a clue to the merging between human and extra-terrestrial life forms. Many of the ancient sites that housed these high-frequency light energies have yet to be uncovered officially in Egypt.

The Tibetans have had a long tradition of working with crystal skulls, although almost exclusively within the monastic setting. Tibetan monks were specialists at working with crystalline frequencies through the harnessing of sound. Selected crystal skulls were housed in caves in the Himalayas, and used by the monks as high-frequency light beacons. Crystal skulls used in Tibet had an exceptionally high frequency, and allowed an extremely high degree of crystalline light bodywork. The Tibetans specialised in building crystalline light bodies that could house the higher crystalline frequencies, and at the same time structure matrices of higher light-frequencies to open new doorways within their awareness. While some of the practices had more practical outcomes, the inner work built up a major dialogue with higher crystalline guides, who, in conjunction with the crystal skulls, downloaded new crystalline frequencies. Access to multiple crystal skulls on the inner planes was commonplace, as was working with many of the principal crystalline frequencies.

Apart from working with crystalline healing energies, the Tibetans also began to explore the energetic relationship between crystalline energy and the inner fire that manifests in our chakra centres as we ascend to the higher frequencies of light. Crystalline light in Tibet represented higher light practices, and was reflected in the physical systems of some of the monks, as their bones became pure crystal that could earth and radiate the higher crystalline vibrations. As this pattern of energy-work developed, the light within became the light without, and a new signal was sent across the land and under the seas, building up an activation with different crystal skulls, such as those found beneath the deserts and the oceans. In essence, the crystalline frequencies housed by the Tibetans, gave them access to the other crystal skulls on the Planet, and enabled them to merge and interact with a number of different skulls. For the Tibetans, the light within became the fire within, and the crystal skulls and crystalline frequencies represented new doorways to explore their inner light.

The role of the crystal skulls in Mayan and other South American cultures is probably better-known than most. Certainly more has been written about it. Rituals involving crystal skulls are well-known, with many different crystal skull artefacts created as replicas of the originals. In some cases, however, the focus was on dark rather than light crystal skull frequencies; with a few exceptions, the focus of Mayan light work did not achieve the same status or light frequency as that of the Tibetans. Nevertheless, limited though their work with light crystal frequencies was, it was sufficient to set up an initial keying-in mechanism for the new Sixth Root Race grid of crystalline light.

Following the prominence of the crystal skulls in previous root races, there has been significantly less activity during the latter stages of the Aryan Root Race. The skulls have been more dormant, and their role and significance have been kept quiet. This is all about to change as the Sixth Root Race emerges.

What is unique about the time we are in now, is the current dramatic shift in the balance between light and dark. At the time of the death of the Avatar Meher Baba in 1969, our planet's energy was divided into 75% dark and 25% light. Meher Baba decreed that by 2069 this pattern of energy would be reversed — 75% light and 25% dark. Today, as the Avatar's nine-point Plan unfolds, we are well on the way to witnessing this reversal. It is important to understand, however, that this change has first to take place in the higher planes, and then filter down through the lower planes, and ultimately into physical form. Consequently, if we were to focus on the physical it might appear that things are getting worse rather than better. Nonetheless, with the astral levels now fully open, as of May 2003, the infusion of mental light into the Planet is increasing rapidly, which means that the doorways for higher crystalline frequencies are now open.

As this change is effected, it is important to recognise the role that both light and dark crystal skulls have played throughout the past root races; and the time has now arrived when it is essential to banish any old patterns of dark crystal skulls which may be held within our physical, etheric, astral or mental spaces. For some, there will have been little or no contact with the dark crystal skulls, while for others the contact will have been much greater and more addictive, so that today there is a need to clear these old dark skull frequencies from our inner spaces. Total commitment to working with light crystal skull frequencies is what is demanded today, and if we are each successfully to make the shift from the Fifth to the Sixth Root Race time-line, then these older, slow frequencies must be excised.

> The stage is now set to re-align and re-adjust the misuse of the past, and to allow the Divine Splendour of the totality of crystal skull frequencies to come through, as the new dawn of the Sixth Root Race rapidly approaches.

Harvesting Ancient Crystal Skull Frequencies

As the new crystal skull frequencies are invoked in Sixth Root Race harmony, love, light and purity, a process for harvesting the old root race crystal skull frequencies has been put in place. This harvesting of old frequencies is most necessary, and includes both light and dark. In order to drive up the vibration of Earth and all her life forms, there is a real need to clear away the débris of the past, and in particular to harvest these old frequencies.

The harvest of light and dark as manifest through old root race practice and ritual, has as its principal focus, the last three root races. This harvesting requires the dredging of old dark crystal skull frequencies, along with the light crystal skull frequencies. For humanity to move into the Sixth Root Race, the song of the light crystal skulls must be significantly amplified, and the song of their dark counterparts banished from our energetic awareness.

It is rather like looking at a cycle of seeding, growth and harvesting of different frequencies through each of the prominent root races.

During each root race, starting with the Lemurians, the crystal skulls acted as the ploughshare that dug up the earth and prepared the way for seeding the new frequencies in matter. They also served as the initiators for sowing the new seeds or frequencies that would drive the formation of each root race. As each root race developed, and the new seeds and concepts were anchored in humanity, multiple light and dark frequencies would be expressed in matter, as souls, through multiple reincarnations and experiences gained in physical form, sampled these frequencies. As the new concepts and frequencies were explored within each root race, the seeds turned into mature plants, and ultimately would be harvested.

This Lemurian cycle of growth from seed to mature crop was repeated for the Atlantean and Aryan Root Races. Today, the seeds of each of these root races have grown into the harvest that needs to be gathered in. Each root race has its own particular flavour, based on the soil and growing conditions and the type of seeds sown on the land; and the harvests comprise both light and dark frequencies as expressed in matter. As each root race cycle is completed in its entirety, the experiences and frequencies gained on all levels must be returned to their origin — to God. The harvest that is now upon us is doing just that — collecting and clearing old root race frequencies.

The harvesting of these root race frequencies has begun, and in the Sixth Root Race time-line it is now complete. However, as other multiple time-lines are shifting from the Fifth to the Sixth Root Race, this harvesting is still in progress. In other words, each individual's experience of this harvesting of old frequencies will depend on where his or her own time-line is, and also on how rapidly we are shifting over to the new Sixth Root Race time-line. Thus, each individual's experience of this process will depend upon where his or her time-line is in relation to the Sixth Root Race time-line.

The harvesters (or, more accurately, combine harvesters) of these old root race frequencies are constructed of group will and intent. Their rotor-blades are formed of the collective foci of light workers; and the power used to turn the rotors is high-frequency mental light combined with Divine Light. Each of the different harvesters is attuned to different frequency-vibrations by virtue of the cutting capacity and size of the rotors. Some of these are directly matched to light frequencies, while others harvest the darker ones. As the harvest proceeds, the fruits will include the crystal skull frequencies from the root races. Once harvested, these frequencies will be threshed and segregated as part of the clearing and extraction of the more ancient, sublime frequencies from the past. The more delicious light frequencies will then form one part of the harvest and be recycled in the formation of the new Sixth Root Race crystalline frequencies.

At the same time, the ancient dark frequencies will be offered up to God as part of the Divine Meal of old frequencies available. This Divine Meal really represents the offering up to God of the different frequencies from the root races, and the harvesting will clear out the old, and will offer up the best of what was sown and reaped in the harvest of the 'everything and the nothing'.

The New Dawn

In Atlantean times, since the focus was predominantly on the dark crystal skulls, the light skulls were forced into the background, into a pattern of isolation and seclusion. This wheel is now coming full circle: a pattern of light crystal skulls is being forcibly introduced into the collective consciousness of humanity, and this beacon of light is beginning to capture the awareness of individuals all over the world. Correspondingly, the dark crystal skulls are now being pushed back, and they will stay back for the duration of time that it takes to stabilise the light patterns and transform Earth's vibration from 75% dark to 75% light. Although by all accounts this transformation will take place by 2069, an extremely short passage of time, it will take many centuries for the patterns of crystalline energy embodied in the light crystal skulls to permeate and become fully reflected into matter on the physical level. So the plan is to bring through a diverse array of light crystal skulls. A large number of them have been on the Planet since their original introduction, and over the next thirty to fifty years there will be a very specific pattern of awakening and re-activation of these ancient crystal skulls.

Crystal skulls are currently located all around the globe, in Russia, Australia, Argentina, Iceland, and central Europe, as well as other key grid-points throughout the Planet. Each skull will be activated according to a pre-selected signature tune that must be generated from the crystalline grid of energy that is currently being downloaded into the Planet. Through accessing many of the crystalline energies from the lower mental planes, and above into the higher mental planes, the correct frequencies will then be activated within the grid to make possible the dénouement of the dark crystal skull practices, and at the same time activate, in true magnificence, the light crystal skulls and their pattern of harmonics.

As these crystal skulls emerge, it will be clear to many light workers, that they have helped shape previous destinies and realities. Today, however, there is a difference, because the frequencies and harmonics within each of them will be re-activated or keyed-in in a slightly different way. The new energies will lead to an activation of an alternate source of light probabilities within the crystal skulls, so those crystal skulls that were active, say, in Lemurian times (and there were a number), will be re-activated with a different "flavour". It is rather like taking an old, delicious recipe for ice-cream, and reconfiguring it with new frequencies from the present, finally coming up with an up-graded, even more delicious ice-cream variety, that exceeds all previous expectations of the old. The shift may be subtle, but the experience will be intense.

So, in the case of the Lemurian energies, these will be re-played with a distinctly new flavour. This will have two prime functions. The first is that it will allow the wash of old Lemurian energies down on the Planet to be cleared and cleansed for one last time over the next few centuries. And secondly, it will allow a new probable reality to form, where the excellence of the old Lemurian energies can be reprised and mixed in with the new crystalline energies of the Sixth Root Race. So it will be like having Sixth Root Race with a hint of Lemurian present, or new Sixth Root Race Atlantean flavour, or Sixth Root Race Egyptian flavour. Each crystal skull that will offer these different energetic permutations will allow a new set of frequencies to be connected into the broadband grid of the Sixth Root Race. Light workers everywhere will be able to access all of these new recipes for future frequencies and future experimentation with these different crystal skull configurations. The possibilities are almost endless.

In practice, the newly-emerging crystal skull frequencies will have a profound effect on all of our psyches. We shall, at one time, feel Lemurian, Atlantean, Aryan, or reflect the different sub-groups within each of these root races. The crystal skulls will throw open the doorways to new probable realities and new dimensions within our awareness, which will, quite literally, take our breath away.

So the Lemurian frequencies of the past reflected a need to bring out into matter, an interplay between light and dark; a need to bridge the animalistic side with the higher side in matter, and to bring through the different spiritual and collective frequencies that were possible at that time. Since the energy levels today are significantly higher than anything that was possible in Lemurian times, the need for reflecting and balancing them is now gone, and the new light-frequencies will make adjustments to these older encodements, and flush them out of everyone's system as appropriate.

So what does this mean in practice? From a crystalline perspective, all of these ancient frequencies will wash through our crystalline bodies as a series of colours, colours that will effectively comprise those colours of the rainbow. With the Sixth Root Race, where the focus is much more on the heart and third eye, the colours associated with those centres will be dominant. Nevertheless, the older colours from the older root races will also be able to wash through our crystalline bodies, giving a subtle blending or flavour to our crystalline essence.

Our crystalline bodies will be able to feel the wash of these energies flowing through them, like a kaleidoscope of colours covering the whole light spectrum, and much, much more. While this may represent what could be termed the basic soup of the day, albeit a crystalline soup, new ingredients will be continually introduced. These ingredients will derive not only from the different crystal skulls themselves, but also from different levels of guidance, including those that are resident within the crystalline halls of light, and within the dreaming spires of the crystalline cities on the inner planes. Every aspect of beauty that is in matter today is reflected within these cities, and it is the crystalline guides that are holding together and beginning to irradiate a new collective frequency of crystalline energy. This collective frequency will represent the final ingredients of the Sixth Root Race crystalline soup. It is too early to specify what those ingredients are, except to say that the focus of attention that is now being directed from the seventh plane towards Earth, will have a significant impact on the evolution of the human race, and on the ability of all of us to fulfil our contracts in matter.

In conclusion, the ancient crystalline knowledge is returning to humanity. Although the levels of expertise attained in early Atlantean times were considerable, there is an opportunity today significantly to surpass what was achieved then. The new energies, and the dawning of the Sixth Root Race, herald unprecedented opportunities to work with the crystalline frequencies of light and love, and to facilitate a merging of the inner crystalline essence with the physical vehicle in an unparalleled manner.

Chapter 7 • The Crystal Skulls and The Cosmic Christ

In the last chapter we explored the connection between the crystal skulls and the last three root races. As these old frequencies are harvested and collected, and added to the Sixth Root Race "soup" of crystalline frequency arrays, the crystal skulls are, at the same time, entering a new-light stream to activate an entirely new frequency of crystalline light for seeding the Sixth Root Race. This new light can be summed up in the words 'total love and bliss'.

The Christos

The crystal skulls, in their alignment with the Divine Will and matrix of crystalline light, are also sending out pulse-beats to other life forms throughout the galaxy. This emanation, this crystalline note of excellence, is first pushing out across the cosmic grid connecting the 18,000 Earths. A new extra-terrestrial frequency is emerging, and it will be seeded into the Planet and into humanity by a new crystal skull.

This crystal skull is beginning to sing its song. It has a shape that is more extra-terrestrial than the human skull, and with a more angular appearance. At its centre is a new matrix of golden crystalline light, which is spinning rapidly and sending out new light frequencies that are being birthed as part of the Sixth Root Race. For humanity the message is simple: open up to the new extra-terrestrial frequencies on the inner planes. Nothing is as it seems, and working with these new frequencies will afford the opportunity to connect with a massive array of new crystalline frequencies from other planets and other worlds.

This new "ET" crystal skull sits at the centre of the grid of all the planets that humanity is working with. This skull is massive and it is sending out a pulse-beat of high-frequency light to the heart of humanity. As the crystal skull sends out its pulse, so humanity will begin to accord and tune in to its frequency in a different way. The golden light of the skull will key into our heart centres, and open a new dimensional doorway to the cosmos. Behind this ET crystal skull stands the Cosmic Christ, or Christos, in all His Love, Glory and Power. The heart emanations that spring from the Heart of the Christos are beyond words, and through this skull will enfold humanity. Golden streams of liquid crystalline light will flow from the Christos into the ET crystal skull, and thence into humanity. Golden light will impregnate our heart centres, as new seeds of the Christos are sown in the hearts and minds of those willing to hear the song, and respond to the pulse-beat of light.

The Christos and the crystalline frequencies of light are but one, as the Christos is the primary initiator, on one level, of all of the crystalline frequencies in the Universe. The Christos is the ultimate crystalline essence, and He reflects all the crystalline frequencies on all planes: the heart of the Christos is the heart of crystalline love and light in its highest form, and this heart activation will always be reflected within all crystalline beings and energies and forms, throughout the Universe. It is like the basic crystalline urge into highest love and purity. As the Christos stands in His Infinity, His Heart will fuel and drive the changes in crystalline frequencies now emerging. Crystalline golden light is emanating from His Heart to all life. These streams of golden light are one part of the new mix of Sixth Root Race love, and they sing of a song of love in all forms, throughout humanity, throughout the 18,000 earths, and throughout the vast range of extra-terrestrial crystalline frequencies, both inner and outer.

These golden streams represent an ancient and utter note of Divine purity, love and excellence. Within each stream of crystalline light are the atomic radiators that helped seed the creation, and which also are parts of the higher vibrations of the Solar Logos. The Solar Logos fuels the sun, which in turn fuels Earth and Gaia, and the Devic Realms. The Solar Logos is also the initiator and pattern-former for new planetary and stellar frequencies. As these streams enter our hearts, they will release a new keynote of bliss and harmony. So as we stand on the edge of eternity and divinity, so it is that these golden streams will open up a new light force in hearts and minds to entertain first within the few, and then within the many, this new keynote of bliss — bliss in eternal light, and bliss in Divine Love. There can be no other perfect alignment for the new Root Race.

As the Christos, the Cosmic Christ, irradiates this new frequency of love, the alignment of crystalline energies within the Planet and our galaxy will shift dramatically. One could say that the Cosmic Christ will take His seat at the Divine Piano, and start to play a new series of stellar and galactic crystalline notes. It will be as if the Divine Piano has been re-tuned in an entirely new way, with new octaves of frequencies raised to a higher range than ever before. The 'high' notes on the Piano will reach a new octave of crystalline love and light: notes that send out a call to each of us on a soul level, notes that heal the soul's separation, and which lend an understanding, at a soul level, that we can be separate, yet connected with the Source — and ultimately with the bliss, love, joy, compassion and beauty that are all in the One. The Cosmic Christ will begin to play this new song on the Divine Piano. The Cosmic Christ, with Heart ablaze, will send out ripple after ripple of crystalline high notes that will echo forth into the ET crystal skull, and ultimately into humanity.

Notes of such serene bliss and exquisiteness of sound will blend in harmonies that will open new doorways, and reveal new layers in the game of love. New harmonies, new melodies will send out a call, and all life forms will have the opportunity to connect in some way with these keynotes of bliss. It will be like angels weeping at the end of time, as the sheer unspoken beauty of the crystalline heart fires the new beginning, the new dawn, of the Sixth Root Race. Hearts will never be the same again, as the elixir of pure bliss, undiluted from the Divine, merges, drop by drop, within the heart song of the Cosmic Christ.

This activation, and the ascending notes of frequencies of bliss, will touch all the crystalline worlds in the universe, as each world in its purity and entirety begins first to resonate with, and then to sing back this song of love. As the pulse-beat echoes out to all worlds in crystalline light, so it is that these worlds will resonate, and their crystalline essence accord with this new song, and embellish it with their own frequencies. As the keynotes of crystalline harmonies combine throughout the galaxies and stars and crystalline worlds, a new type of song will emerge, with bliss, harmony and love as the initiators and the focal points. The song will resonate throughout the Universe, and the full force of this new crystalline heart love will touch everything in its path. No heart will be untouched as the feathers of love and the wings of delight begin to unfurl within the crystalline essence of complete purity and profound bliss.

This Divine Song of crystalline bliss will, in love and purity, ignite the crystalline fire. Just as the keynotes of higher crystalline light have been the liquid elixir, so it is these new frequencies will form a new beginning, building a crystalline fire, as new crystalline flames of light burn all that goes before it. These flames of love and light will purify all life forms, and will provide the basis for a new fire within. The crystalline fire of the Cosmic Christ will begin to burn our hearts in an entirely new way: a new fount of love, a new fount of utter bliss, will form in the emptiness that the crystalline fire will leave in its wake. This crystalline fire will roar through our centres, much as a forest fire, when the wood is dry and there is no moisture. The crystalline fire will burn hearts and minds, and where before the liquid light of crystalline light held us in light, this will be superseded by the crystalline fire of pure light essence and love.

As the Cosmic Christ plays the keyboard of the Divine Piano, the whole Piano will begin to change in frequencies, so that spectrums of light will flow through its clear crystalline essence. As the Piano turns golden, and then to a golden-white frequency throughout, the crystalline fire will be ignited within the central ET crystal skull which the Cosmic Christ is forming. This timeless formation of the crystal skull houses the essence of Love from the Cosmic Christ. The fire within the crystalline essence of the skull will become ignited, and the crystalline light will burn in the flames of purity. As the Piano comes alive with this crystalline fire, which is then downloaded into the ET crystal skull, the new crystalline flame will race into Earth, and then out into the crystalline worlds and galaxies. This crystalline fire will purify the worlds and stars, to usher in a new level of love and a new level of crystalline seeding.

The ET Crystal Skull

The opportunity exists, first for the few, and then for the many, to merge with the ET Crystal Skull, as a means of tapping more directly into the crystalline fire of the Cosmic Christ. This is not something that can be rushed, and it can only be attempted when the call comes from within: this call will be heard in heart, not the mind, and then only in the true silence of the Divine Heart. Both the song and the call will be soft at first, like a golden drop of dew whispering upon the first sunlight of the day. The heart will know when to answer the call, for the song will swell within, and as it becomes more insistent, the focus of intent will begin to change as the golden streams of crystalline light begin to spin within the dimensions of the heart.

New heart will begin to form in golden light, as the personality will start to negotiate the twin peaks of bliss and despair. Bliss in one moment will be followed rapidly by despair in the next, as the personality struggles to find attunement with the new heart vibrations. The subtlety and softness of these new vibrations should not be underestimated — they house layer upon layer of new frequencies of crystalline love.

In the fullness of time, the heart will be ready to hold these new frequencies in the moment, and to begin to key into the ET crystal skull. The heart will dictate when the time is ready to connect with this crystal skull in the inner planes. The source and activation of this skull are from the seventh plane, and with the Cosmic Christ energy acting as the transformer fuelling its irradiation, merging and melding should be done in stages. The ET crystal skull will first form in the heart, as light-streams from the Cosmic Christ prepare the way. As the merging with this skull develops, the dimensional space within the heart will expand to a massive degree, as the frequencies of bliss and love are downloaded. The heart will expand and expand, and as the inner silence builds, the crystal skull, once the preparation has been completed, will send forth a pulse, a spark of crystalline fire, which will ignite within a new focus of love. The fire will build and build, until the whole of the heart centre is burning — burning in crystalline light and crystalline fire. All will be consumed within this fire — nothing will be left. The space within will then be open to the true seeding of golden bliss and love from the Cosmic Christ. The vortex of golden energy that was within the crystal skull can be downloaded into the heart. Crystal skull will merge with golden heart in totality, and the Cosmic Christ will be present within the dimensionless space of the heart.

This connection will be most profound as the vortex of golden light begins to spin to a new dance of crystalline light. As golden streams spin out from the golden vortex, the merging with these new frequencies of bliss, unconditional love and utter purity will form a new platform within the crystalline heart. The inner dawn of a new crystalline heart will have begun, with an ongoing pattern of profound and sublime merging with the ET crystal skull and the Cosmic Christ. The dance of a million loves, a million kisses from the Divine, and the total silence in unity sublime, will herald the true merging in the heart of crystalline fire.

The Divine Crystalline Fire

Once housed in the heart, the crystalline fire will begin to spread throughout the body to the different centres, and within the body organs and tissues, especially the bones. It will burn all of the centres, leaving nothing within, and elevating them to a new source of purity and harmony. Chakra centres will be perfectly aligned, and with each one on fire, there will then emanate from the crown chakra a pillar of crystalline fire. This pillar will connect with all of the centres, from base to crown, and as the crystalline fire builds, the bore of the pillar will grow as the crystalline energies within the spine and brain expand. As each centre becomes consumed by the fire, there will, quite literally, be nothing left in them.

As the Divine Fire purifies the hearts and minds of those willing and able to sustain the purification and re-alignment, the new crystalline frequencies of the Cosmic Christ will reconfigure the Divine Inner Highways from the physical to the inner crystalline essence. All will be utterly transformed. As the pulse-beat of golden crystalline light reaches out through the inner planes, and fires and re-structures our crystalline bodies, the frequency-vibrations that they can house will ascend accordingly. Within the physical realms, our centres will be cleared, and our crystalline light bodies will also be re-structured and re-wired, to hold and earth the new Christ crystalline frequencies. As this re-alignment takes place, the broadband of new frequencies that are being gridded around our world will also be transformed. Golden crystalline light will pour down into humanity from the Divine Piano through the crystalline superhighway. As the frequencies comprising the superhighway ascend most dramatically, the time for turning inward and invoking our Divine Inner Call will have arrived. The sea of crystalline frequencies that will flood down the superhighway will infuse and restructure the frequencies of the crystalline matrix of light. This matrix will ascend and ascend, as the Cosmic Christ plays the divine crystalline melodies.

The Divine Crystalline Fire will spread throughout the crystalline matrix of Divine Light that surrounds the planet. This matrix will be transformed as the crystalline flames first purify and then build new frequencies into it. The octaves of crystalline notes from the Cosmic Christ will be directly transposed into the crystalline matrix, as it becomes a matrix of crystalline fire. The crystal skulls that are gridded into the matrix will also be changed by the new, ascending frequencies, and the crystalline fire will realign the light-frequencies within. It will be as if all of the high crystalline frequencies have a new focus of crystalline fire: beneath the crystalline light will be the crystalline fire as it houses the ascending crystalline octaves of the Cosmic Christ Crystalline Light.

Once the crystalline matrix surrounding the Earth has been transformed, then these new crystalline frequencies will spread out into the solar system, the galaxies and beyond, in the form of a wave of high-frequency crystalline light which holds the keynotes of crystalline fire. The light without will become the fire within.

Angelic-Crystalline Frequency Notes

While it is fair to say that the utter bliss and sublime love embodied in the frequencies of the crystalline Divine Fire will be like no other, the opportunity for invoking new 'hybrids' of this type of energy will also arise. One of the more specific experiments in new frequencies will involve the inter-relationship between angelic and crystalline light. These house different permutations and harmonics of light, although both represent extreme high-frequency light.

As high frequency light, angelic light is principally found in the higher planes, primarily the fifth and sixth: angels as they leave the seventh plane are awoken in one of these two, and following this activation they spend time gathering inner-plane experience — angels usually only incarnate on the Planet for one lifetime, and this occurs after a huge amount of experience has been gained on the inner planes. Although angels can hear the Father's Call, and can answer Him, they are never able to see Him. Their one lifetime in physical matter affords them the opportunity to do this, before returning to Divine Bliss.

As the crystalline vibration ascends in response to the infusion of Divine Light from the Cosmic Christ, there will also be the opportunity for blending and merging the higher crystalline frequencies with the higher angelic ones. A new form of light will be birthed: angelic-crystalline light. This will hold the frequency-notes of both the angelic and the crystalline energies, but will merge with them in a new way. As the angelic wings of timelessness beat to a pulse of angelic will and intent, so the crystalline fire will fuel the angelic light, and birth a new Divine Mixture of love and light.

The Cosmic Christ and the New Order

As the Cosmic Christ begins to irradiate His Love and Light into the crystalline essence of the ET crystal skull, the tidal wave of Divine Golden Energy that will sweep through the Earth, and out into the galaxies that populate the Universe, will re-activate and re-align old dimensional doorways. These doorways will call back into our awareness a Divine Stellar Cartography that has been lost for thousands of years. This Divine Cartography was elucidated in the distant past, during the late Lemurian period and early Atlantean period. It was also re-discovered and re-worked by the ancient Egyptians. For the most part it has remained hidden from us, and it is only now becoming re-discovered because the old dimensional doorways of the past can be re-accessed in a new way. Apart from re-opening these old doorways, the new energies will also birth new ones, and in particular a major one which will open in the very near future. The birth of this new galactic doorway was foretold long ago; the repercussions will be immense.

Our planet is surrounded by a blue ring-structure known as the 'ring-pass-not'. This ring of blue energy seals off the planet from a range of different energies, and all incarnating souls must pass through it. The ring acts as a block or filter to all previous soul memories, and all souls passing through it forget who they are and where they have come from. Hence, most people mistakenly think that this is the only lifetime we have. The new energies entering the Planet, combined with the will and intent of those working with the light, are now establishing new dimensional doorways that can pass through the 'ring-pass-not', and provide access to the extra-terrestrial frequencies that lie beyond.

So as dimensional doorways are built though the 'ring-pass-not', the possibility for downloading new extra-terrestrial informational matrices now exists. In this particular instance, these matrices can be likened to maps of the cosmos, each one representing a different series of frequency-notes. In the ensuing sections, we shall briefly explore some of these different frequency maps, setting out an initial seed or imprint for the stellar cartography which is to come, and which will be anchored more directly into the Planet by the star children. Three types of map will be described — the Grand Map, the Angelic Map and the Crystalline Map. In one way, these maps will represent the new order in matter, as the new souls entering our world will firmly fix their intent on these new frequencies, and radiate out to the rest of humanity a new understanding of life.

The Grand Map

The Grand Map, as it is so called, reflects the full wheel of life: the 18,000 earths, and all the solar systems within the Universe. It is important to understand that this master map is not a physical representation of the Universe, but a dimensional representation showing the inter-relationships between all aspects of the 18,000 spokes of the wheel of the grand-life. The map is like a grand overview, and it shows the progression of spiritual evolution from the outer rings of the wheel, all the way through to the centre, where planet Earth is located. The map itself cannot be understood within a two-dimensional context: it must be accessed through a series of keys or holograms, which provide access through specific doorways. This map can only be understood from within, and not through external form.

The star children who are now seeding the Planet have each been provided with specific parts of the map. These smaller maps are like the grid co-ordinates of our ordinance survey maps. The Grand Map covers the world, while the smaller ones cover specific grid areas within these maps. The challenge facing the star children is firstly to understand their own maps, and to recognise that the frequencies which they house are reference points and sign-posts to unlocking their own individual cosmic map; and secondly to seek out other star children who have similar, matching maps. In forming a collective unit with other star children, the ultimate aim will be to build up a grand picture of the

Universe, where each star child will have his or her own map, and where thousands of these will be joined together to form the Grand Map in physical matter. As the star children recognise their own maps, and then recognise others of their kind who have similar ones, the next challenge will be to work out where their particular map fits into the grand scheme of things. This will require extraordinary trust and clarity of purpose, guided by a deep sense of intuition and rightness. Trust in this intuition is essential for these star children, and it is the principle reason why the parents need to be open, and to ensure that the intuitive pulse in their loved-ones is not shut down through the appliance of ignorance or misunderstanding.

If this project is successful, and this remains a fairly big 'if', then Earth will house in physical form the first representation of the Grand Map. The recognition, realisation and energy that will be released in this process will form a core component of the Sixth Root Race in the future. The fundamental, physical recognition of the Wheel of Life, with the 18,000 earths and all of the dimensional doorways connecting the different stellar and planetary systems will mean that Earth has become the Grand Beacon, the Grand Communicator of Life in the Universe.

The Grand Map then functions as the over-arching series of frequencies. Beneath this umbrella, there are sub-sets of frequencies that can also be explored.

The Angelic Map

There are a number of different ways in which these subordinate star maps can be accessed, depending upon one's dominant vibration or essence. For those light workers who have a principle essence derived from the angelic realms, the star maps will house a series of specific angelic frequencies. The dimensional inter-relationships between the planets and the stars will be different from access points such as the crystalline energies.

Angelic maps provide information about the angelic realms, and the journey of different souls through them. Angelic frequencies are extremely high, and have as their starting-point a focus of the Divine Will as manifested through their thoughts and actions — angelic energy is a form of heart energy, blended with the Divine Essence of the Father's Will. Preparations for the incarnation of large numbers of angels are being made, and as with the star children, these angels will hold within their energy systems a portion of the angelic map. It will become apparent, with time, that there will be an unfolding and exquisite communion and energetic interplay between these angelic children and the Christos. It would not be too far from the truth to say that they will also carry an aspect of the ascending frequencies of the Christos as they manifest into physical matter, although in a somewhat different way from the crystalline frequencies.

Angelic children will house a stunningly high vibration, and will bring with them a focus and intent second to none. As angels, they will have one lifetime in physical matter before returning to the Father's Bliss. This means that they will generate a massive energy-wave of angelic light and love on the Planet, ensuring a quantum ascendancy in planetary vibrations. The angelic children will also begin to establish — in a similar way to the crystalline grid, albeit in a less developed form — an angelic grid of frequencies that will surround our world. The children will plug into this grid of angelic light, and will begin to build a deeper connection with their angelic essence, although in truth, because they will only have one lifetime in physical matter, this connection will not really be necessary, except on a superficial level. They will have within their energy systems the means to access directly, and without any interference from past-life frequencies in matter, their angelic essence. Direct and dynamic access to the angelic essence inside each angel child will be available, and the role of light workers today who hold and house specific angelic frequencies, is to prepare the way for the angelic babies to access their angelic essences directly.

One of the difficulties facing these angelic babies is that after the extremely pure and high vibrations of the fifth and sixth planes, the grossness of physical matter will be a major shock to them. It will be important to allow their nervous systems to develop safely, and then to permit the inner angelic light and information-flow to be accessed directly, for locked within their systems will be the angelic maps that will birth into humanity an entirely new series of frequencies. Just as the crystalline formation of Divine Essences have as their primary focus the Divine Crystalline Piano, so the angelic frequencies will be played out by the Divine Father on the Angelic Harp of destiny. The angelic frequencies will be the harp-strings, and the harp will be formed of highest angelic light. As the Divine Father plays the Angelic Harp, so the frequencies will be directly downloaded into the angelic babies, and seeded into the Planet.

The angelic notes as expressed through the essences of these babies will establish the angelic grid surrounding planet Earth, which will begin to come of age, as angels-in-matter walk her surface, and sing the song of the Divine Father. Angelic wings of huge dimensions will begin to grace the Planet, and to house new frequencies of angelic bliss and love, as these reach a new crescendo of Divine Light and Love. As with their crystalline counterparts, angelic frequencies will house different notes or octaves, although of a more refined nature. These notes can be captured or sensed through angelic colouring, where the vibrational essence of the angelic babies can be colour-coded to show their family or angelic status. The angelic colours will sweep through this planet like a whirlwind of light, as they spread and diversify within physical matter. Angelic golds, blues, indigos, peach blossoms and aquamarines will simply take the breath away as these delicious frequencies pull at the heartstrings of humanity, and pluck new melodies of love within there.

This angelic wash of frequencies will complement and mirror in a profound way the crystalline frequencies of the Cosmic Christ. The golden glow of Christ Energy will suffuse and wash through the angelic frequencies, similar to two patterns of energy wrapping around one another, forming a double helix of light and love; the angelic frequencies will form one strand of this helix, while the crystalline vibrations will form the second. As the helix turns according to its inner geometry of perfection, the angelic and crystalline frequencies will form an entirely new energy-type. This divine angelic-crystalline essence will seed a light beyond description, combining the angelic focus with the crystalline intent, merging the angelic heart with the crystalline pulse, and driving an accord of angelic-crystalline love and bliss to entirely new heights on both the inner planes and in physical matter. The heart of the angelic host will be tangibly fused with the heart of the crystalline essence, as the principal energetic merging takes place within the double helix.

As this angelic-crystalline double helix of Divinity unfolds, it will be imprinted into the etheric and physical DNA of those that can sustain this new vibration. In the fullness of time, the new babies will automatically house this angelic-crystalline vibration within their physical systems, but until then, there will be few who will be able to accommodate this new vibration of inner bliss and light.

As the frequencies of the angelic-crystalline double helix merge in union, each helix will be capable of housing and expressing different angelic and crystalline keynotes, so, not all angelic-crystalline helices will be the same. Rather, each will express an array of different angelic and crystalline frequencies that give each its own signature and series of frequency-notes. For example, some helices may contain angelic frequencies of blue and indigo, while the crystalline focus may be golden. Similarly, the angelic frequency may be more pink and gold, which will be combined with a deep blue crystalline vibration. As these different permutations and helices build, there will be opportunities for these angelic-crystalline helices to house multiple frequencies, and to blend totally new formations from the underlying angelic and crystalline energies. The results will be, quite literally, heart-breaking: and as the hearts of humanity are shattered, they can then be reformed and re-built within a completely new stream of angelic-crystalline light and bliss. The angelic-crystalline heart will then have come of age.

The Crystalline Map

In one sense, the crystalline maps represent the true science of stellar cartography. The new star children house within their systems a considerable amount of crystalline light, and inner knowledge of crystalline energy. The maps held by the star children convey information covering the inner crystalline spheres and the crystalline worlds that are manifest throughout the physical universe. As with the Grand Map, these star maps provide information on crystalline doorways and access points in space, so that they do not equate directly with the physical maps of the galaxies.

The maps show the crystalline systems as points of crystalline light combined with lines or connecting crystalline tunnels or doorways. As the Sixth Root Race evolves, the crystalline maps will evolve, and will be re-structured according to the dictates of the Cosmic Christ Energy. New portals of crystalline light, and new geometries of crystalline harmonics will be introduced between different stars, planets and galaxies. Crystalline light will diverge, and the light of the crystalline fire will replace, and blend with the liquid elixir of crystalline light.

The realities created by the different star maps will be under-pinned by specific crystal skull frequencies. Each skull, if it is focused on these extra-terrestrial frequencies, has the capacity to create a star map. So one crystal skull can create one set of star maps, while another, with a different frequency, has the capacity to create an alternate crystalline star map, with a different set of linkages, as if viewed through a different pair of crystalline spectacles. The crystal skull 'glasses' therefore create the crystalline maps, and the relationships and connections expressed within them.

What this means is that for each light worker the maps may appear different, although it may be that they are all looking at the 'same' map, but with a different focus. This highlights another important property of the star maps — their probabilistic nature. The doorways built into them represent lines of probability between different realities, and depending upon one's sympathetic alignment, these will unfold in different ways. Thus an angelic interpretation of a given star map will present a different reality in terms of order from a crystalline representation of the 'same' map. It is also possible to have multiple interpretations of crystalline maps. Multiple, probable realities are the order of the day, and this is one of the things that make the grand experiment with the star children so interesting: no one knows how it will turn out, what the final, collective, unified map will look like.

So, as the star children incarnate, become activated, and are gridded into the crystalline matrix of Divine Light, they will begin to access their inner star maps, and to focus on the underlying crystalline energies that underpin such maps. The results will be extremely interesting, as different realities or multiple realities become matched up with their corresponding multiple reality.

The Triple Helix

The bringing-together and merging of the angelic-crystalline frequencies will create an entirely new energy platform for our world. With the double helix housing the angelic frequencies in one strand, and the crystalline frequencies in the other, there remains the opportunity to add a further strand of energy, to create a ***triple helix***.

This new strand of frequencies will be represented by the Devic frequencies and their energetic expression in physical form. The Devas represent the life forms that are present in all physical matter, whether they be mineral, plant or animal. Devic frequencies are like the glue that holds together the matrix of physical matter, and within the human context it can be visualised as being a rat-like figure inhabiting the human body. The rat has whiskers and a tail, and embodies the basic pattern of physical life necessary for housing the soul. Devic energies are really the substance of physical life.

Until now, the Devic focus in human beings has been driven by slower frequencies, so that the Devic life force has been quite dark. This energy pattern is now changing, as the Devas themselves evolve, and ascend in frequency. In human beings this can be represented by the shift from a dark rat-like appearance into a white rat appearance. This escalation of frequencies within the Devas will continue, until eventually the Devic light will be of an extremely high frequency, and will take on a more golden hue, to mirror the crystalline frequency-vibration. However, this pattern is still some way off. For the present the main focus of the Devic energies will be to evolve to the white pattern, and then to build this light frequency into a higher and higher pattern of light. As this scenario unfolds, there will be an opportunity for the Devic frequencies to merge with the angelic-crystalline frequencies, to generate a new light-stream in matter. The double helix of the angelic-crystalline frequencies will merge with the Devic helix to create a new platform of light frequencies. The energy housed in this triple helix will be unique, and it will impact upon all three frequency platforms. The triple helix will therefore unify and house three main frequency types — angelic, crystalline and Devic energies.

The importance of this Divine merging of major frequencies cannot be overestimated. The Devic energies, manifested in all life forms, must be transformed and raised so that the underlying vibrations can host the new crystalline and angelic frequencies entering the Planet. Devic energy feeds upon experience, and as its frequency ascends, it needs to be able to feed upon higher-frequency energies. The changes impacting upon the Planet are open to all life forms, and the transformation in Devic energy will ensure that they take place. A new type of Devic heart is emerging, as light workers begin to tend their inner and outer gardens of expression. New frequency-matches are taking place, as light workers with crystalline and angelic frequencies begin to match and merge with the Devic energies. There will be great joy at this union, as the love and intent expressed within the Devic heart will open new doorways within these light workers. Again, ancient doorways of knowledge and experience will be opened up, as older aspects in matter are reclaimed.

The triple helix of angelic, crystalline and Devic energies will be completely new to our world. As each helix rotates around the others in a Divine play of love, the triple helix will represent a new doorway within the Planet. This doorway will house a frequency bandwidth of astounding depth and breadth. It will contain a new type of love: we have considered the transformation in crystalline and angelic energies, and the transformation in Devic frequencies will be no less monumental. Devic heart and Devic love will be totally re-structured, and as we access our hearts within, so this new doorway will show us a new kind of love in Devic light. It will be a love that will, in one sense, be no less profound than that of crystalline and angelic light.

In the last chapter we explored the energetic relationship between the new crystal skull frequencies and the Cosmic Christ, and the impact that this would have on all of our energetic systems. For some this new vehicle of energetic excellence will be accessed relatively quickly, while for others the process will take longer, depending upon the strength of their energetic and nervous systems, and the focus of past-life work. As the Sixth Root Race experiment begins to unfold, the re-emergence of the crystal skulls into humanity's consciousness is assured. Connecting with the skulls in the physical can be an extremely beneficial part of this process, and can help develop a deeper connection with the skull frequencies.

There are at present a limited number of physical crystal skulls available, including the Mitchell-Hedges skull, the British Museum skull, and the Texas skull — known as Max. Each of these presents a different bandwidth of energy, and houses different frequencies. For example, the Mitchell-Hedges skull has a narrow vibration that goes straight up, while Max has a broader vibration that goes outwards. The current limitation in access to so few physical crystal skulls is likely to change rapidly over the next thirty to fifty years: ancient crystal skulls are waiting to be found in parts of Australia, South America, Russia and China, and as these come online, it will only be a matter of time before they make their physical presence known. For example, it is said that a crystal skull will be uncovered in Australia:

> The signal of this . . . crystal skull is very high, very focused and extremely narrow, in that it captures a perfect alignment of crystalline geometry as expressed through sound and light.

In this chapter we shall explore some of the outer manifestations of the crystal skulls and the crystalline frequencies, in terms of inner and outer reference-points. The Sixth Root Race experiment is as much about anchoring these new frequencies into physical matter as it is about exploring the probable realities embodied within the crystal skulls on the inner planes. Around the Planet, there are now emerging a number of physical sites that are beginning to call to humanity in general. These are either high-frequency sites that are already active, or sites that are in the process of being activated. They are like crystal beacons in the night, and as night turns to day, their significance and their role will become more clearly understood.

The Sixth Root Race also demands that we embark upon a grand inner journey, to begin to understand who we are and where we come from. While this is something of a grand tour, and very much beyond the scope of a book of this kind, we shall take a few shorter excursions internally, to give the reader a series of inner access points which will help put into a slightly different context some of what has been said so far. These excursions will not only have as their focus certain inner-plane structures or spheres, but will also include a reprise of some of the more important light-frequencies that were explored in the previous three root races. These focal points will include what is known as the Circle of Twelve; the Dolphin Oceanic crystal skull; and a new seeding of crystalline energy through crystalline acorns, that has already started to take place. In addition, a description of several other skull frequencies will be included as a means of both initiating a dialogue, and providing examples of the scope and focus of these different frequencies. The aim will be to provide a starting or initiation point to some of the new frequencies, and to the dimensional doorways that can access crystalline energy.

The Crystal Beacons

As has been indicated, the crystal skulls are an integral part of the crystalline grid that is beginning to surround our planet. This grid needs generators to maintain the high-frequency energy, and those generators are the crystal skulls. Up to six crystal skulls will initially be used to initiate the basic grid, followed by six more once this has been established. The skulls will act as transmitters of high-frequency crystalline energy, like giant crystalline beacons.

At certain points around the Planet, huge crystalline beacons of high-frequency light are being seeded and established. The first of these was erected in Cancun, Mexico, at the beginning of 2003. As part of this seeding mechanism, a massive crystal skull was brought down over the land: its dimensions etherically — over 500 km high. This skull has now started to transmit an energy-pulse that is radiating from its centre as a wave of crystalline energy. The pulse-beat is initially slow but over the years to come it will become much more rapid and intense.

The position of this crystal skull in Mexico is important, because the geography of the region resembles the dish of a radio receiver. The skull is at the centre of the dish, which is helping to amplify the signal. The area around Cancun was used in ancient times, particularly dating back to the Mayans, as a location for high-frequency crystalline energy; and although the amount of work carried out there was limited, the initial seeding for today's crystalline pulse was in fact initiated in Mayan times.

It will take up to 19 years for this site to become fully active, and during this time slow-frequency energy will be cleared, and the ground energy will rise to a much higher frequency. Once this process is complete, the crystal skull will send out its operating pulse-beat of Divine Light and information for all those willing and able to pick it up.

A second crystalline beacon was established in Switzerland in the latter part of 2003. At an ancient battle site, near the Oberalp Pass, a second crystal skull was seeded and activated. As with the first skull, this one will act as a powerful transmitter of crystalline light and all who pass within its energetic radius will be affected.

Other giant crystalline masts will be erected over the coming years, providing a crystalline network of Divine Beacons. These will send out their crystalline pulse-beats, and like light-houses will act as points for attunement and direction.

Seclusion Hill

If one were to identify one principal point on planet Earth that acts as the master generator, then this would have to be Seclusion Hill in India. Seclusion Hill is situated at Meherazad, Maharashtra State and the ground energies there are extremely high. To visit Seclusion Hill is to connect with the highest crystalline frequencies on the Planet.

Seclusion Hill was especially significant to Meher Baba and His Universal Work — He would spend long periods of time there, in a wooden cabin that was purpose built for this Work. For most of the time He would work in isolation, hence the name of the site.

Seclusion Hill is intimately linked with Meher Baba's Tomb at Meherabad, and the two sites manifest an incredible energy pattern: the Father's Energy, which is manifested in His Tomb, covers all of the planes. One way of visualising this energy exchange is to express the Father's Energy in the Tomb as being an inward movement, while on Seclusion Hill it is expressed as an outward focus: it goes directly up.

Seclusion Hill represents the focal point for the birthing of Sixth Root Race energies into the Planet. It is a gateway to the crystalline realms, and to a huge crystalline city on the inner planes. This crystalline city resonates at such a high vibration that it is not visible to the naked eye, but can be seen clairvoyantly. Its vibration is unique, and it is sourced from the seventh plane. It houses an enormous array of structures and energies — halls of learning, gardens of crystalline perfection, and special crystalline sanctuaries all form part of this enchanting citadel. A huge diversity of rooms and structures can be accessed within, including vast stores of information on human and Earth development; on the inner planes and on how natural law operates. The key to accessing this information lies in working more and more closely with our guides.

This crystal city is also an access point for a group of higher-plane guides who are seeding and preparing humanity for the new Sixth Root Race frequencies. These guides originate from the seventh plane, and they function as God's administrators in this new dawn.

Seclusion Hill is therefore a dimensional doorway to the emergence of Sixth Root Race frequencies, and it provides access to the highest planes, including the seventh. (It is also possible to connect with other crystalline cities on the inner planes through meditation. While Seclusion Hill provides the closest access point on the Planet, other crystalline structures can be accessed once you have established a good rapport with your crystalline guides).

There is a strong pattern of beautiful crystalline energy at the Tomb and also in Baba's Hut, which is situated directly next to it. Beneath the Tomb, it is possible to connect with different patterns of crystalline energy, and through projecting one's awareness under the physical Tomb, these energies can be felt more directly. Since the physical Body of the Father is buried in the Tomb, there is also a pattern of crystalline energy that remains in place from His Skeleton. Baba's Hut also has a strong pattern of energy, and here also it is possible to focus in the ground beneath it, and tune in to the crystalline energy within. As with the Tomb, the frequencies are exquisite.

It can be instructive to focus on different crystalline places on the inner planes. In the higher planes, there are crystalline cities which contain the unity of crystalline light, and which provide a structural reference-point to particular plane levels. It is possible, through meditation and working with the crystalline guides and crystal skulls, to find and explore these cities, and to experience the beauty of crystalline light and its representation on the inner planes. Alternatively, images of the cities are sometimes presented directly in meditation, without any formal requests. Their form can take the breath away; and to see the crystalline turrets of these crystalline cities can be stunning.

Another important place on the inner planes is the crystalline cave that houses the crystal skulls. This cave has been referred to in a previous meditation (Meditation to Work with Specific Crystal Skulls). Inside are arranged hundreds of different crystal skulls, each with its own particular frequency and crystalline beauty. The cave is a storehouse for the skulls, and a point of activation for each skull frequency. By entering the cave and connecting with a crystal skull, the individual begins an activation sequence for that particular skull.

Other inner-plane structures and spheres may come to you in meditation; and it can be extremely helpful to keep a diary of your experiences, so that after a time you will see a progression of events. This will also build your confidence in what you experience, as you may be given information about events and experiences to come, which subsequently come to pass.

Having considered some of the different focal points of the crystalline energies and crystal skulls, we shall now explore more specifically the focus of working with multiple crystal skulls, and especially the Circle of Twelve. An initial platform for connecting with these new frequencies was set out in The Meditation to Work with Multiple Crystal Skulls.

The Circle of Twelve

At the end of Chapter 5, a meditation for working with multiple crystal skulls was described. In this meditation, twelve skulls were called in, and used as an initiation point for working with a range of crystal skull frequencies. The number twelve has its own significance, directly related to the circles of the Avatar and the Perfect Masters. The Avatar stands at the top of creation, and below Him are arranged 81 circles of His disciples. Each circle contains twelve disciples, each one standing within another circle of twelve. It is like a hierarchy of circles, where the first twelve forms part of the next level of twelve circles, and so on, each unit of twelve 'begetting' another twelve. These circles can also be visualised as rings.

The circle of twelve crystal skulls is significant, in that it represents a ring of crystalline excellence and a pattern that reflects the Divine Order. Each skull within the twelve will reflect different qualities and attributes, so that, for example, one crystal skull may denote 'power', another one 'love', another one 'purity', another one 'wisdom', and so on. The combined frequencies of these skulls make up the whole, or the One. Depending on which of the twelve is invoked, the range of frequencies expressed by it will be a direct reflection of the One or God.

Working with the circle of twelve represents an extremely powerful keying-in mechanism to a range of different skull frequencies. Although some of this information on the circle of twelve goes back to previous root races, the focus now must be on expressing the excellence and purity of vibrations that are available at the start of the Sixth Root Race. Working with the twelve will open up ancient doorways within your psyche and sub-conscious, allowing a massive flux of information to be recaptured. The analogy that comes to mind is "multi-dimensional" living. With the twelve, it will be as if you are standing at one moment in a desert, with a crystal skull in one hand, reflecting on the focus of the ancient Egyptians. At the same time you can be with another skull, working in ancient temples, keying-in different love frequencies from the stars. Or you can be in the mountain ranges of Tibet, working in crystalline caves of glacial purity, expressing the light within. The twelve can establish this pattern of multi-dimensional crystalline living in unique ways.

As you connect and merge more deeply with the circle of twelve, you will start to build your own ring of crystalline light. This ring represents power, it represents your commitment and oath to working with the light, and it represents a different kind of access point to working with the crystal skulls. It is like an inner doorway. As the circle of twelve forms around you, and your vibration builds, the ring will focus upon your heart. The circle of twelve, as a ring of love, will be **within** the heart. As this happens, you can invoke for multiple keys, and for access to a new, inner crystalline doorway, for as the circle of twelve spins and radiates within your heart, the ring that forms will open a new door with a crystalline key that will form there, expanding as it does so. The key is of pure light crystal, and exquisitely formed. Once it has stabilised within your heart, the new crystalline doorway can be accessed, and as this builds within your heart, the circle of twelve will surround it.

The doorway represents a new portal to crystalline light, and a new ability within your energetic system to work with the crystal skulls and crystalline energy. First and foremost, the vibration of love that the doorway represents will bring about a new ascendancy within your energetic system. Access to the higher crystalline vibrations on the higher mental planes will be much easier, and will provide you with a new platform for earthing and holding the new frequencies.

As the doorway stands within you, you may sense the crystal skulls from the circle presenting themselves one by one in the centre of the doorway. The keys to these twelve skulls will then be placed in different chakras and will set a new standard in your energetic system. (Although there are only seven main charkas at present, part of the future development of our energetic systems will include an expansion to twelve chakras). While the focus of the twelve may vary for each person, the list below is an example of the energies that the twelve might manifest. The roman numerals relate to the crystal skull number.

I Power

II Love

III Harmony

IV Purity

V Innocence

VI Will and Intent

VII Wisdom

VIII Unity

IX Bliss

X Light

XI Heart

XII Soul

It may be that for various people the focus of energies represented by the circle of twelve will be different. For example, in contrast to the types of energies expressed in the list above, a different circle of twelve would focus predominantly on different frequencies of love, and would consequently bring through a range of different love frequencies.

With the crystalline door in your heart, and with the twelve keynotes of crystalline access to the door, the next stage is to go through it. Behind it is an ascending stairway of crystalline steps, all representing different frequencies. The stairway stretches up into the light, and as you start to ascend the steps, you are stepping-up your frequency. The energy from each step is absorbed as you ascend, and it may well require several months of practice to master the frequencies of the steps and reach the top of the stairway, but once this has been successfully done, you will find yourself standing at the doorway to a crystalline temple. The temple is beautifully crafted of pure crystal, with different crystalline energies and frequencies housed within it. As you enter, you will see in the centre of the room a crystalline casket containing a pure crystalline body that has the same image as yourself. The crystalline body is utterly transparent, and is a manifestation of your inner crystalline essence. It also represents your crystalline divinity.

As you go towards the crystalline body, it may be that you stop and just look at it, and as the pattern of energy builds, the crystalline body may merge with you: either you go towards it or it comes out of the casket towards you. As your bodies meet, just allow a complete merging and alignment to take place. Your whole body will feel crystalline, and will be utterly clear, without any blemishes.

This is a significant pattern of alignment, which represents an ever-deepening pattern of merging with your crystalline essence. Merging like this is similar to stripping off layers, so that you can go on merging deeper and deeper as layer after layer is stripped off. As the merging becomes more pronounced, the love and the light that will enter your system will become stronger, more profound, and silent. It will be like merging with an ever-increasing expanse of crystalline energy.

This clear pattern of crystalline energy is but one aspect of an ascending set of frequencies. It is rather like the base line. It is important for our on-going Sixth Root Race alignment, but it is also important to recognise and be open to the changes that can and will take place within our crystalline essences. A developing pattern that will emerge is the massive impact of the energies that will be pushed through from the Cosmic Christ into the ET crystal skull and into humanity. The golden energies of the Cosmic Christ will transform and re-align our crystalline bodies. So, with time, as we connect with the Cosmic Christ, this golden pattern will start to be reflected in our crystalline essences. The crystalline body, originally clear and transparent, will start to take on a golden hue, so that while remaining clear, it will become subtly golden in colour. New vibrations and rays of light will begin to be sparked off within it. The eyes within the golden essence will also turn a deep gold, and will blaze forth a light-frequency that is pure crystalline love. The golden crystalline light within the crystalline essence will build in intensity, and at the same time, the heart centre will turn a deeper and deeper gold as the frequencies build. This means that the Cosmic Christ frequencies will now start to be earthed in earnest within our physical spaces; and as we merge with this ongoing pattern of crystalline Cosmic Christ Light, the energies will build powerfully.

By going through the crystalline doorway and into the temple of our inner crystalline being, we shall have consciously established a direct connection with our crystalline essence. This recognition is an important part of reversing the fragmentation of our systems that has arisen through our spiritual journeys down into and through matter. This energetic pattern will also enable us to align our energies more easily with the exquisite higher frequencies that will now come in.

A further development may also be possible within the temple setting and the constant merging with our crystalline essence: with time, it may appear that the roof of the temple disappears, and is replaced by the night sky full of stars. The star maps of the night sky will not necessarily be recognisable as those we can see from Earth, but the stars, and the frequencies that they represent, will be the calling-card of the other crystalline extra-terrestrial frequencies that are calling to us now. As the stars call to us, our crystalline essence may begin to expand skywards to meet them. As this take place, a deeper union with the crystalline worlds and diverse frequencies will be possible. An analogy for this is that of the Divine Father playing the Divine Crystalline Piano, and reaching a massive crescendo within the symphony, in which cascades of notes and frequencies are sent forth into the silence of our inner divinity, where, with a suitable inner space, we can begin to access these notes and harmonise with them. As the notes cascade in inner space and time, the crystal worlds that you may have inhabited, and the stellar crystalline frequencies that you will have acquired, will wash through your crystalline essence like a kaleidoscope of colours. The effects will be profoundly moving, and will help you to reconnect at a deeper and deeper level with yourself.

It is important to recognise that these signposts to the inner crystalline essence, and the ever-deepening connections that we can make with it, are not simply journeys in and of themselves: for the pattern of merging will go on, and the foregoing is an attempt to give a sense of how these deeper mergings may feel and to suggest ways in which they can manifest in your consciousness. It may well be that the presentation of deepening energetic exchanges will manifest within a different framework, which is moulded by your own past experiences and connections with crystalline light.

The Dolphin Oceanic Crystal Skull

The dolphin energies represent a collective extra-terrestrial frequency that has been with the Planet since the Lemurian time period. They have been extremely important to the Planet, and in particular to the seeding of new frequencies within the oceanic realms. The need for higher-frequency light, and it's earthing within the sea, is just as pronounced as on land. On one level the Dolphins have acted as guardians of specific frequencies, and the time is rapidly approaching when their collective frequency will ascend quite dramatically.

The seeding-mechanism for this ascension will work through a particular crystal skull, known as the Dolphin Oceanic crystal skull, which houses a distinct set of blue frequency-vibrations of extra-terrestrial origin. The inner-plane setting for the emergence of this skull is best described by analogy. Imagine a sea of crystalline silver which is utterly smooth, the smoothness and silvery opalescence extending down in to the oceanic depths. Situated at the bottom of the ocean is an exquisite aquamarine blue crystal skull, whose shape is different from anything that we have encountered before — it rather resembles the shape of a dolphin skull, but at the same time retains some human features. It is rather like looking at a hidden pattern — if you look at it one way, it looks more dolphin, and if you look at it another way, it resembles more the human form. As you focus on the skull, it begins to rise to the surface of the ocean, and eventually lifts out of the water. This reflects the activation sequence that will take place in the future, initiated by an ancient keeper of the crystal skulls.

The frequencies that will be expressed by this crystal skull will be quite different from the ET crystal skull, and from other skulls known to us. The skull will 'talk' directly to the dolphins, and will enhance their communication: one of its key roles will be to bring through a more direct connection between humanity and the dolphins, and it will focus on building a deeper merging of the respective energy systems of humans and dolphins alike. This will be important for the seeding of the future root races beyond the Sixth. The dolphin vibration brings with it a collective heart frequency, and a joy largely unmatched in humanity. In addition, the aquatic environment has helped the dolphins to develop new forms of communication, and to build up information about oceanic depths untapped by humanity. In order to bring about a union of land and sea in a new way, the human and dolphin energy systems will need to merge. The new frequencies of the Sixth Root Race must permeate the oceanic depths containing the vast myriad of life forms. In the distant future, as the Planet becomes covered with much greater tracts of water, through the formation and expansion of seas and oceans, the specific frequencies mastered by the dolphins will be extremely beneficial to humans.

The new root race that will supersede the Sixth Root Race will blend some of the specific dolphin energies with the human frequencies, and the body-form that will thus be generated will borrow certain aspects from the dolphin anatomy, both subtle and physical. The Dolphin Oceanic crystal skull will start to work with this new pattern of merging, and will pave the way for a much deeper and more dynamic communication and communion between humanity and the dolphins. There will be much rejoicing as the two come together.

The Blue Extra-Terrestrial Crystal Skull

The embodiment of this crystal skull is, quite simply, galactic love. Its frequencies are the culmination of harvests of different love vibrations that are out of this world, and they represent all the most beautiful and harmonious of the collective extra-terrestrial crystalline frequencies. The skull emits a deep blue colour, within which there are gradations of other blues, much like the transition from a blue sky to the onset of the evening sky before twilight, followed by the deep, dark, blue velvet that is the night sky. The blues in this skull are fathomless, and they hold the keys to a huge array of love vibrations. The purity of this love is unmatched, in that it is taken from the essence of crystalline divinity, and sings a song of layers of love in the unfolding of God's Divine Grace. This skull is, quite literally, like a key to the Divine Heart.

The shape and formation of the Blue ET skull is different from that of the normal human crystal skulls, having more of an angular, extra-terrestrial look: the eyes are larger, and set deeper within the skull, and the cheekbones are higher. To connect with this skull in heart and third eye is to call in Divine Love at its purest: a love that is untainted, a love that calls out to the all. As the connection is made, the deep blue frequencies will overwhelm heart and mind, as the depths of blue unfold the different layers of love. The liquid blue crystalline light is an elixir of love frequencies at their highest, and it will sow in the hearts of humanity an understanding of the scope and bliss of different types of love. The pulse-beat of the Blue ET skull has started to sing out — gently at first, but over the next few years, the call will become louder and louder.

Crystalline Acorns

The crystalline acorns represent, on one level, the seeding of new Sixth Root Race crystalline frequencies within our awareness. They have been formulated by our crystalline guides and the crystal skulls, and will be seeded into the Planet by light workers over the next few years. The initial operation will be to seed them in a few light workers, who will then spread them far and wide.

Through working with their crystalline guides, light workers will be able to access the acorns, bring them within their space, and then retain them for future planting in the hearts and minds of those willing and able to listen to the crystalline song. At the same time, each light worker impregnated with these seeds will develop a new pattern of crystalline light, and their crystalline light bodies will house a different flavour of crystalline energy.

The crystalline acorns represent a potent seeding-mechanism, and they house a matrix of crystalline light and love that will grow into crystalline oak trees. As the acorns grow within each person's energetic system, they will bring about a new pattern of growth, featuring a new root system and the development of a trunk, branches and leaves. The roots will grid the individual into the crystalline matrix of Divine Light, rather like an electrical plug, and give access to the crystalline energies that are being gridded into the planet. The growth of the oak will focus on the development of branches and leaves that will have very specific functions.

As the acorns grow into full-blown crystalline oaks within the energetic systems of those initially seeded, the call of the trees will, within the few, form a collective harmonic of crystalline light. The multiple gridding of these crystalline trees will form new crystalline forests, which will, in turn, produce more acorns to be distributed around more of humanity. With time, and with the human body-form playing host to these crystalline giants, the crystalline forests will then be found in locations all over the Planet.

As the crystalline oak trees become activated within people's energetic systems, several things will happen. Firstly, the branches and leaves of the trees will act as transmitters and receivers of crystalline energy from different realms and spaces. They will receive crystalline signals, sent out by crystalline guides on the inner planes, that will then be grounded within the physical space of the individual. The crystalline branches will also turn and face the stars, and begin to pick up the extra-terrestrial crystalline song. The song will reverberate within the leaves, and the trees will sway and dance to the new crystalline tunes. As the crystalline frequencies bombard the planet, the crystalline leaves will pick them up and download them into the physical. The diversity of frequencies being picked up will escalate rapidly once the forests are established. Ultimately, these forests will act as massive receivers to the extra-terrestrial crystalline song, with each forest tuning in to a different song that nevertheless reflects the collective medley.

The second effect will be that the crystalline leaves and branches will harmonise with and respond to the crystalline winds of timelessness that run up and down and through the crystalline matrix of Divine Light. These winds will grow stronger as the crystalline harmonics and frequencies within branch and leaf sing their own songs. The winds will whisper to the leaves, and the leaves in turn will reply as the focus of light builds. The trees will shine brighter and brighter as more and more crystalline light is downloaded into them.

It will be important that the roots of the oaks be well grounded in the physical shell of light workers carrying these trees. The signal and frequencies will build, and once the storms and vortices of light get downloaded into the crystalline matrix from the Cosmic Christ and the ET crystal skull, the crystalline grid surrounding the Planet will resonate, and impact upon the crystalline oak trees that are connected into it. New frequencies of light and love will pour down into the leaves, and where before the crystalline light had been powerful and bright, the frequencies of the Cosmic Christ crystalline light will be as a supernova of golden starlight. The crystalline oak trees will be utterly transformed.

Expressions of Crystalline Divinity

What all of these different frequencies will do, each in its own way, is to bring about a new platform of crystalline light that holds the diversity and beauty of crystalline energies in heart and mind. As humanity begins to link hearts and minds, and the light replaces the darkness, so the crystalline vibration of Divine Love will connect and unite us all. Within the beauty and joy of the new crystalline frequencies, there will be opportunities for people to re-discover different expressions of crystalline divinity. For example, a new breed of crystal singers will emerge, as light workers of old rediscover their ancient crystal voices. Heart and mind will merge in the expression of new crystalline notes of perfected sound. The closest approximation today can be heard in the voices of some opera singers, although the resonant vibration of crystalline energy can be found in other musical forms. As crystal singers of old, light workers will recognise that the truest pitch of sound is that which is found in silence, and which can be held by focus and attention, and drawn into their space.

Crystalline frequencies will also be expressed through art, in writing and in healing. New patterns of crystalline healing will develop, where the etheric and physical systems can be re-wired and re-structured according to the new crystalline frequencies being gridded into the Planet. Crystalline guides will work through these new healing patterns. New methods for dealing with musculo-skeletal difficulties can arise out of working with the crystalline substance of bone. Healing frequencies will also be directly downloaded from those who have the capacity to house the higher crystalline energies. Ultimately the crystalline light bodies of the crystalline healers will be able to download directly a new matrix of light into those receiving the healing energies; and where there is compatibility between healer and patient, the potential for a merging between the crystalline light bodies will be explored.

Deeper crystalline connections will also be built up in more mediumistic work, allowing direct channelling of crystalline guides and the crystal skulls. Direct access to the skulls on the inner planes will also be possible once the inner crystalline highways have been built. The information that is available to humanity from the crystalline spheres is immense, and direct access to it will help forge a deeper understanding of the Divine Plan as it unfolds. Access to these higher-plane guides will also require a significantly larger internal space to house these energy beings, and the new generation of mediums will need to reflect the changing inner pattern, for the new guides will embody an entirely new type of energy. As all of these expressions of crystalline divinity evolve, the heartfelt resonance of peace, divinity, bliss and joy will be felt in the hearts of all those involved.

Other types of crystalline work will also be on offer. Clearing the Planet of older, slow-frequency energies remains a top priority, and those with the expertise, and with systems able to cope with rescue work, will be needed. Rescue work represents a pattern of energy-management that allows souls that have passed over, but who remain trapped in the earthly realms, to be directed back to their holding-pattern on the inner planes. Millions of souls remain trapped on the Planet, because the manner and emotional pattern of their death have made it difficult for them to move on. This 'taking up' of trapped souls to a point where they can re-connect with their incarnatory programme is extremely important.

Nor is this rescue work limited to Earth. Although the new crystalline energies can act as a 'net' for trawling for lost souls on Earth, the focus of those working directly with crystalline energy means that rescue work of a non-terrestrial origin will also be possible. Once the pattern of clearing on Earth has reached a certain level, the net will spread out to other worlds where extra-terrestrials souls trapped in matter will have the opportunity to be called in, and led to a greater point of balance.

Other ways of expressing crystalline divinity will also be possible. Painting the new crystalline forms, and downloading the high-frequency energies in colour, will give people an intuitive reference point to crystalline energy. The formation of new colours that can physically represent the range of different crystalline frequencies will be highly significant.

Similarly, the music harmonised with the higher crystalline frequencies will open people's systems to the recognition of a crystalline signal within. Such music will operate from the higher chakra centres, and it will need to download the necessary frequencies from the higher planes. There is a limited amount of music that can do this within a crystalline setting today, and there is a need to expand on this pattern, so that heart, third eye and other centres can respond to the new frequencies.

As the frequencies ascend dramatically with the infusion of the Cosmic Christ energies, the divinity and bliss felt within will be second to none. The ideal of 'Heaven on Earth' will come to mind, as the Sixth Root Race crystalline light drives up the planetary vibration, and begins to sing a song of unity, harmony and love with other keying-in frequencies, such as those from the Angelic and Devic realms. The new children, as bearers of new crystalline, angelic and stellar frequencies, will ensure that what starts as a small drop of Divine Love, will very rapidly escalate to cover the whole Planet. The crystalline acorns within the energetic systems of those working with crystalline light will build forests of oaks that will act as beacons for galactic light. The new gridding of crystal skulls within the Planet, and their activation as power generators of crystalline light, will raise the frequency as these beacons of Divine Light call in the Cosmic Christ Energies. The golden energies of the Cosmic Christ will then establish a new pattern of crystalline energy: crystalline fire, that will purify all life forms, and burn the slow frequencies out of those willing to listen to the new song. These energies will, in turn, usher in a new heart of love in humanity, and a new accord of bliss in golden crystalline light that will have no equal across the universe. Golden crystalline light will be the new beacon of Divine Delight.

Ⓐll that has been said so far about the different crystal frequencies, and how they will manifest within the Planet as part of the Sixth Root Race formation, hints at an underlying crystal skull essence. The analogy of the Divine Piano is at once most relevant here. As Meher Baba plays the Divine Piano of crystalline elixirs, and sends out the frequency-vibrations of exquisite crystalline harmonies, the notes and melodies are preparing our systems for even deeper transformations than those previously discussed. These are likely to occur further into the future. The previously-described changes in our frequency-vibrations are in themselves profound, and the new frequencies embodied by the Cosmic Christ will have an especially massive impact on all of us: but what is being hinted at here is an ever on-going, ascending host of new frequencies, that will build on this deep transformation process. One way to imagine this is not as a normal three-course meal, but rather as an exceptional nine-course banquet. The reference to the nine courses reflects the focus of God's nine-point plan for the initiation of the Sixth Root Race during the one-hundred-year period from 1969 to 2069.

In this Divine Scenario, God is the Proprietor of the restaurant of 'the everything and the nothing'. Different groups of humanity sit at the tables of Divinity that are spread throughout the restaurant. Other groups work in the kitchen, cleaning the dishes, preparing the vegetables, and assisting the chefs. Special chefs, identified and selected by God and His Maitre D' of Divine Light, are preparing the different courses, with the Perfect Masters helping to oversee the operation.

The special courses forming the banquet can be listed as follows:

First course: The crystalline hors d'oeuvres

Second course: The soup of eternity

Third course: The Cosmic Christ
Fourth course: Mast love
Fifth course: The Galactic Skull
Sixth course: New Soul Light
Seventh course: The Dragon Light Dessert
Eighth course: Chef's Surprise
Ninth course: Chef's Surprise

The Early Courses

First course — The crystalline hors d'oeuvres: The new infusion of crystalline frequencies that has begun represents the hors d'oeuvres. They will involve accessing the new crystalline frequencies and the crystal skulls. These are like a smörgasbord of different frequencies, which can be sampled as we wish and within the tolerance limits of our systems.

Second course — The soup of eternity: The next course will be a special soup, which is being prepared specifically by God, the Divine Maitre D' and the Perfect Masters. This soup will be unlike any other, and it will have a richness of flavour and a thickness of frequency that currently match everything that is and everything that has been. Careful selection of spices and ingredients has also been supervised from on high. A cup of this soup of eternity and beyond will have an effect on the diners like no other. The soup will be a surprise, and it will represent an indescribable new wave of energy. The soup will set the standard for the following courses.

Third course — the Cosmic Christ: The third course represents the second substantial wave of new ascending energy and will be the next transformation of our systems in their totality, once the effects of the soup have been digested. This course is being driven by the new infusion of Cosmic Christ Energies through the ET crystal skull and, its impact on humanity, and in particular those open to the Cosmic Christ Energies, will be utterly devastating in a most positive manner. Heart centres will never be the same again, and the ascendancy of vibration will demand that we change the way we focus and hold these new energies. A new ruthlessness in holding and earthing emerging frequencies will be demanded. If the energies are not brought down and then expressed in an appropriate way, they will simply turn in on us — with negative consequences for our health and our mental stability.

Expressing these new energies means finding our operating frequencies within the context of a suitable form of practice. Some of us will be the new generation of healers, some will be the new artists and sculptors, some will be the new writers, and some the new singers. Whichever path of expression we take, it will be extremely important to follow our hearts, and to sing the song in whatever way is appropriate.

The new frequencies that will sweep through the Planet, including all life forms on it, and then continue out into the solar system, galaxies and the universe in turn, will be unimaginable, and they will drive a massive shift in our consciousness and awareness. People have talked about the Second Coming of the Christ, and it has always been assumed that this would be in physical form. In reality, the manifestation of the Cosmic Christ Energies will represent this Second Coming. Love will be the keynote.

As humanity digests this course of the Cosmic Christ over many lifetimes in matter, the timing, impact and effect of the Cosmic Christ frequencies will dictate the timing for serving the next course. God's Divine Maitre D' will be orchestrating the timing of the next course.

The Fourth Course — New Mast Frequencies
While the Cosmic Christ will have called into matter a new series of love vibrations, with an underpinning of unconditional love, the fourth course will manifest a different type of love frequency. The primary initiators will be the 'masts'. Masts are God-intoxicated souls who, although in physical matter, have an awareness so turned inwards towards God, that they have little or no concern for outside stimuli and life in general. To those who do not recognise their energy systems, they

may appear to be insane. The reality is very different, since these masts express and bring through a unique type of light and love that is formed through their devotion, their purity and their deep love of God. Masts have only one interest, and that is to look at the God within, in utter devotion and love. They have no interest whatsoever in the external world, and their behaviour reflects this stance.

During His Life on Earth, Meher Baba spent a considerable amount of time seeking out and meeting masts in India, and during these meetings He would electronically re-wire them for future lives. Once the Cosmic Christ Energies have resonated through humanity and the 18,000 earths, the way will have been set for the re-incarnation of many of these masts. Meher Baba will personally supervise this new wave of higher souls descending into matter.

Each mast as he or she incarnates will have a massive amount of inner light and purity. Waves of high-frequency light will accompany this new descent of specialist souls into matter. The masts will be more focused on the outer world than previously was the case, and their role will be to take the new frequencies that have been set into humanity, to earth them within their DNA matrix, and to become living, walking resonators and transmitters of various series of different crystal skull frequencies. Each mast will house a crystal skull within a heart that has been infused with specific frequencies of light from the Divine Father. This will be like the Father sitting down at His Divine Crystalline Piano, and conceiving of an entirely new way of expressing and forming music. So where there had been say, classical piano music woven through time with the high notes and beauty of master composers, the shift will move to a new format of musical genre which will form the basis for an entirely new wave of musical expression. It is rather like talking about the shift from classical to pop, although the frequencies being referred to here are somewhat different and much, much higher.

As crystal skull frequency-radiators in matter, and with direct connection with the Divine Father, the masts will set about building new doorways and dimensional alignments with God in humanity's inner space. Imagine our capacity to connect with the Divine Frequencies as being symbolised by an aerial. The aerial has a size measured by its height and width, a specific composition that will vary from aerial to aerial, and a design that is wedded to the types of signals that it needs to receive. All of these variations will give rise to different types of aerials, all reflecting our different abilities to connect within. In those places where, following the input of Cosmic Christ Energies, there had been a modern aerial hewn out of golden crystalline light, the masts will come along with massive boosters to upgrade and strengthen the signal in a substantial way. Humanity's connection with God had already been upgraded to high-frequency broadband through the previous courses, and it will now be realigned with high-frequency Divine broadband with God's personal and direct line. The bandwidth of love will be incredible.

The masts will infuse a new light into humanity and this fourth course will be most rich in the new frequencies of love. As humanity begins to merge with the new mast frequencies in matter, the recognition and connection with a deeper love of God will become manifest. Mast light will enfold and encircle humanity in an entirely new way.

As this meal is digested within humanity, old systems and ways of doing things will drop away. Current business and banking practice will be transformed, as the masts become the new business brokers of the age, brokering love as the new currency of exchange.

The Fifth Course — The Galactic Crystal Skull

While the masts will have helped to anchor a new love within the heart of humanity, the fifth course will have a distinctly different flavour. A way of describing its underpinning frequency is to call it 'Galactic Skull'. Again the Maitre D' will time to perfection the arrival of this dish, as the waiters harmonise the service to all guests, taking care to ensure that all receive their portion at the same time, there will be something of a collective gasp as the plate-covers are removed: for the fifth course will comprise an individual galactic crystal skull for each and every diner.

This galactic skull will connect everyone who can digest its frequency with the galactic wheel of life and the 18,000 earths. Each individual galactic skull will be a collective manifestation of all galactic skulls, so that each one will be *the* 'Galactic Skull'. Another way of looking at it is to say that the 'Galactic Skull' will divide itself into individual galactic skulls for all to connect with. The crystalline frequencies of the galactic skull will supersede all that has gone before, and will represent the driving mechanism for the end of the early phase of the Sixth Root Race and the transition into its middle phase of evolution. Instead of the focus being on crystalline fire as driven into humanity through the Cosmic Christ, the next phase will call in an entirely new concept of crystalline energy, which contains within it a culmination of the merging-together of the angelic, crystalline and devic frequencies with a new galactic light. This galactic light will embody a new source of soul fusion, and represent the love vibrations from the seventh plane in a totally new way. Since each soul has its origins in the seventh plane, this fifth course will call into play a brand-new focus of soul evolution.

Each soul, once it becomes separated from the Ocean of Divine Bliss, undergoes a process of further segregation. It first splits into seven main aspects, each of which then divides into two identical soul aspects. These two are known as twin flames, since they are made of identical energy, and are an exact replica of each other. There are therefore fourteen soul aspects in all. Only five of these are allowed into physical matter at any one time, and when any of them meet in matter, this represents a meeting of soul mates. Soul mates will radiate between themselves a very specific and powerful array of frequencies that will speed up their evolutionary process. Given that there are six billion people on the Planet at present, the chances of meeting a soul mate are extremely rare. It is even more rare for anyone ever to meet his or her own twin flame, since this represents the perfect match. Twin flames express a soul love that is second to none.

However, the new frequencies of the Sixth Root Race are sending out a call for soul aspects to meet in physical matter, a process which is part of the plan to drive up the frequency of everyone's energy systems at this time, prior to taking this connection to a much deeper level, coupled with the new energies of the Sixth Root Race elixirs of light and love.

As the Divine Flame of crystalline light burns through humanity, the Galactic Skull will call into matter a new form of soul light that is directly sourced from the Over-Soul. The Over-Soul is the holding mechanism for all souls, and can be visualised as resembling a giant mushroom without the stalk. The mushroom shape reflects the Over-Soul, and suspended from It are the many millions of souls in evolution. The Over-Soul represents the next level of depth of connection with God, and while the previous courses in the Divine Banquet have focused more on the soul level, and on the infusion of different light-frequencies into each soul aspect in physical matter, the fifth course will focus on driving a new wave of energy down from the Over-Soul into each soul aspect. This will be used to generate an even deeper wave of collective and unified energy within the crystalline frequencies of fire and light, and the new Galactic Skull will act as the initiator, soul reservoir and generator of the frequencies required to bring about this next step in soul evolution.

In basic terms, the Cosmic Christ Energies represented the infusion of a new form of crystalline fire into humanity, while the masts represented an infusion of new love frequencies into matter. The Galactic Skull will build on these twin frequencies of fire and love, and bring about a whole new transformation of soul light that will be effected by the coming-together in matter of multiple twin flames. Within the Galactic Skull, there will be a pillar of Divine Light that houses all the frequencies of light and love that have gone before, both terrestrial and extra-terrestrial. This will be presented to those souls advanced enough and willing to receive the new galactic energies. Twin flames will be drawn to this pillar of Divine Light, and as they connect in matter, and ignite a new pattern of burning within their respective systems, the Divine Light embodied in the Galactic Crystal Skull will represent a frequency around which they can begin to merge and ascend together. Like moths before a light, the twin flames will start to circle around the pillar of Divine Light, and dance to an ever-deepening array of mergings. As twin flame begins to merge with twin flame, Divine Union will be the order of the day.

The process by which twin flames come together and merge is known as twinning: union of the heart within, union of soul light in pure harmony, and union of the fire within as it is absorbed into a new soul essence. Twinning is union of all that is within the twin flames, the merging of all soul experiences in the fires of the Divine Heart, and the bringing-together of twin flame love. The Galactic Skull will reinforce this union and unity of heart, as the frequencies break new ground of love in matter.

What this new course represents is the birthing of a new soul love on the Planet, where those souls that have undergone sufficient preparation will be able to withstand the force of love that is presented through meeting one's twin flame. The Galactic Skull will infuse those twin flames with the galactic light of the Divine in an entirely new way, so that the fire of the Cosmic Christ Energies will be combined with the love frequencies of the masts as initial supporting mechanisms, to house the love vibration of the merging of true soul essences.

As part of this process, the Galactic Skull will be infused with a brand-new series of light-frequencies from the Divine Piano. For this fifth course, Meher Baba has restructured the Divine Piano of crystalline light. It still houses the elixir of crystalline frequencies that are played out on the crystalline notes, but He has also re-designed the Piano to contain a new pattern of soul light. So where before the Piano held all crystalline essences as connected through the different soul aspects, the new version is now plugged in more directly to the Over-Soul, giving a new depth and pattern to the crystalline arrays. Over-Soul light now fuels the Divine Piano.

The coming-together of twin flames in the new galactic light will bring in a new platform of love frequencies into matter. It will represent a new form of merging or twinning forged in the Divine Heart of soul light, and particularly the unique light of twin flames merging and becoming one. As these twin flames come together, they will begin to ascend around the pillar of light within the Galactic Skull. The crystalline fire and Divine Light of the pillar within the Galactic Skull will draw in the twin flames of unity and union, where new frequencies of love can connect with the soul within, and with the Over-Soul above. The twin flames, in spiralling around this pillar of light, will ascend, and in this ascension, will call in the light of the Over-Soul. Where before only the light of the soul could be accessed, it will become possible to access the light of the Over-Soul, and to call it into physical matter. New Over-Soul frequencies will be forged into physical matter to open new inner doorways of Divine Love within. The standard of twin-flame love, forged through twinning in galactic light, will call in these new frequencies of Over-Soul love, light, collective harmony and Divine Unity. Unity is the new dawn of light; unity is the dominion of dragon light, and the ascending stairway to Over-Soul light.

The Soul and Over-Soul

The fifth course, like all those before it, will represent a major shift in soul and planetary evolution. The patterns necessary for invoking and calling in the new soul light, and deeper connections between soul and Over-Soul, are being initiated at the present time. More and more soul-mates are finding each other, and beginning to understand what the term 'soul-mate' really means, rather than the more superficial definitions that are often used incorrectly. Similarly, the evolutionary platforms, forged in multiple experiences in matter, which are necessary for twin flames to meet, are being established; and in certain circumstances the connections are being made in family circles. Soul-mates are meeting and living together, and where appropriate, further soul aspects are being called into the emerging family unit. In special circumstances, twin flames are being called in. The energetic mixes where two or more soul-mates come together are extremely special, and with the added energies from the connection of twin flames, the possibilities for speeding up soul evolution are manifold. The energies generated through having two, three or more soul-mates living under one roof are especially potent.

While little has been said of the connection between soul, Over-Soul and the Divine, the presentations of these different levels are but stepping-stones between soul aspects in matter, the soul and soul family alignments, and the Over-Soul. The building of bridges in matter between the physical vehicle and the subtle bodies on the inner planes represents the beginning of the new crystalline dawn. As the Sixth Root Race unfolds in ever-widening circles of Divine Light, the connections between the physical vehicle and the higher aspects or higher consciousness will become deeper, as will those between the soul and the physical vehicle. Since the soul desires diversity of experience, the connection that has to be made between the physical vehicle and the lower self must be forged with intent and will, so that the higher self and the soul respond appropriately. The focus today should be on ascending to new octaves of light and love. By bringing together the lower self and the higher self, and by forging direct links between the physical vehicles and the subtle bodies all the way through the etheric, astral and mental levels to — ultimately — the soul levels, the bridge of higher crystalline frequencies can be established. In a way, this represents the opening part of the Sixth Root Race grand experiment.

The diversity and unity of love and light in physical form, which are watchwords for Sixth Root Race intent, also concern the alignment and re-alignment of different souls, and their grouping within soul families, and the higher connections with the Over-Soul. As we have seen, the soul can be divided into fourteen aspects. The underlying frequency of love between these different aspects will form the bedrock of Sixth Root Race love. A part of the experiment then will be to expand this soul-love frequency within different soul families, so that ultimately, different soul aspects from different soul families can stand side-by-side, and yet merge in the unity of a new pulse-beat of love. The Sixth Root Race vibration is seeking to create many, many more soul-mates, so that the soul-love frequency can spread between a whole host of soul family groupings. This will have a dramatic effect in amplifying the love frequencies in matter, and in creating new soul groupings that are simply soul-mates in frequency. These new soul formations may have come from different souls, and they may or may not be from the same soul family, but they will all uphold a specific love vibration that is common to all soul-mates. This brings a new meaning to the terms "group", "collective", since the love vibration is soul love, a much higher expression of love than that normally expressed in matter today.

So, the grand experiment is seeking to create new soul groupings. These new alignments can also be explored between twin flames: the love frequencies expressed between twin flames can be used as a standard for the new platform of love vibrations between different soul aspects from different soul families, so that these different aspects can begin to build the higher love frequencies required for twinning or twin-flame merging. Experimentation with this new pattern is beginning to be explored in matter, as souls who have been in incarnation for long periods of time, and who have the capacity to build new love frequencies, can begin to explore more profound levels of merging. In one sense, the merging between twin flames is the highest expression of soul-aspect merging, and by aligning with and anchoring to these higher frequencies, there is no reason why different combinations of different soul aspects from different soul families cannot attempt a similar merging or twinning. Once the karma, personality, mind and everything else has been stripped away, the merging of God's light-sparks in a Divine Union of bliss and love represents an ultimate form of love.

As the Sixth Root Race experiment continues, the focus upon deepening the connections between different soul aspects will shift to the construction of new frequency highways between soul and Over-Soul. The imprint of new energies from the Galactic Skull will usher in this new phase. The new alignments created by the merging and unity generated through soul love and its distribution through different soul families, will set the platform for the next phase of soul evolution. The Over-Soul represents the higher connection with God. It is, if you like, an aspect of God. The frequencies housed in the Over-Soul are higher than those held in the soul. By building new connections from the soul to Over-Soul, and especially from souls that are effectively twinned, and large groups of souls and soul families vibrating as soul-mates, the accord and harmonised frequencies will build a new bridge of soul light to the Over-Soul. In one sense, there is always a progression of energy from the Over-Soul to the soul; there also has to be a directive of information sent out from the Over-Soul to the underlying souls to create this shift. However, once an alignment has taken place at soul level, it is possible for the bridges to be built, and for new soul and Over-Soul highways to form in sublimely high practices of light and love. It should be recognised throughout this, that the light and love frequencies that we are talking about are incredibly high.

The middle phase of the Sixth Root Race will focus, then, on these soul-to-Over-Soul highways of light and love. Because the Over-Soul encompasses all souls, and also their soul aspects in living matter throughout the Universe, this new platform of energy will bring about an entirely new unification and collective harmonisation of living frequencies. Group and collective frequencies will be increasingly emphasized and expressed in hearts and minds, as the Over-Soul forges a direct current with the soul, and the soul forges a direct current with physical vehicles. The link between physical and Over-Soul will be assured.

Because the frequencies included in this fifth course of the meal are especially powerful, it will take humanity some time to digest it. It will also take time for this process to be seeded into humanity. Nevertheless, while this is going on, preparation for the next, the sixth course will already have started.

The Sixth Course — New Soul Light

The sixth course is somewhat different from the previous courses, and it reflects a specific infusion of soul light into matter. With the restructuring and re-formulation of the soul families and the soul-to-Over-Soul highways, the structures and patterns are now in place for a direct infusion of new soul light. The sixth course, then, is this new soul light, and it is rather similar to a cold ice cream or digestive, which helps digestion of the previous courses. The range of new frequencies that will be introduced in this Sixth Root Race Divine Banquet will be massive, and for humanity the focus will mutate into something entirely different. By the sixth course, the song of the Sixth Root Race is well established and this course represents an opportunity for all previous courses to be properly digested, while at the same time introducing a new quality of soul light into humanity. Meher Baba has overseen the preparation of this new light. This course marks the end of the middle period of Sixth Root Race development, and is a prelude to the final three courses, which include the sweet desserts and much more.

The Final Three Courses

At this stage, it is difficult to give much detail about the content of the final three courses of the Divine Banquet, because such massive changes will have taken place in humanity. At the same time, the experimental nature of all that will have taken place make accurate prediction difficult.

The seventh course — The Dragon Light Dessert: It is likely that the seventh course will be an extremely particular and special course — a one-off, although in a sense all of the courses in this Divine Banquet are one-offs. The seventh course will be a special kind of dessert, created out of Dragon Light. This Dragon Light Dessert will represent a collective pattern of light frequencies that have existed beyond eternity, and were among the first to be formed following the initial separation from the Divine. The focus of this course will be to access these extremely ancient frequencies, and to connect with the collective vibration that Dragon Light embodies. The song of the dragons is already calling to us, and as our frequencies ascend in matter, there will be opportunities to begin to connect with this new type of light. Dragon Light calls in eternity as it is forged in the ring of love and placed within the heart.

The eight and ninth courses — *Chef's Surprise:* Following on from this seventh course, there will be two more courses that have yet to be finalised. The analogy is rather like having a selection of possible desserts, fruits and cheeses on offer, and until the dessert is served, it is difficult to know what will be selected. In addition, the timing of the serving of each of the courses is extremely important, and will be controlled by the earthing of the new frequencies in matter. By the time the desserts are selected, these will represent the late-stage development of the Sixth Root Race.

The frequencies on offer in the Divine Banquet of the Sixth Root Race are without parallel, and they will help to build a pattern of light and love where it can truly be said that 'Heaven is on Earth'. The deeper connections and new dimensions of love frequencies between all of humanity, and the transmission of these energies to all life forms throughout the Universe, will reflect a huge transition from where we are today, and indicate what the Sixth Root Race will embody in thousands, and possibly millions of years to come. There is no other Divine Experiment like it, and while God has invoked the changes, and set up the energy patterns and starting-mechanisms to make the transformation possible, it is still up to humanity to embrace these changes, and to partake of the Divine Banquet. God can only make the suggestions, and since we live on a free-will planet, we have the choice of whether or not to follow His Wishes.

So, the Divine Banquet has started, and the first course is being offered. All who wish to partake of this Divine Banquet are invited to the restaurant of 'The everything and the nothing', and asked to find a seat. As the first course is being served now, time is of the essence, because it will be rapidly superseded by the second and third courses. As the frequencies embodied in each of these courses are transformational at extremely deep levels, at soul levels, it is necessary to be present to receive them in the correct order. It will not be possible to swap the courses around, and there will be few opportunities to accept late-comers who join in once the main courses are underway. Special dispensations will be required.

It goes without saying that the beauty, enormity, magnificence of what is being seeded in the Sixth Root Race is without precedent: it offers humanity an enormous spiritual opportunity to forge a new evolutionary pattern at the soul level. It offers the opportunity to live with, day in, day out, new love vibrations that will expand to fill our hearts in every way. We shall be blessed beyond our wildest dreams.

Chapter 10 • The Crystalline Heart

For the most part, as indicated at the start, the focus of this book has been upon the third eye rather than the heart centre. However, it is important to recognise that crystalline light and crystalline love are also heart-focused in a most profound way. In this final chapter, the aim is to explore some of these different expressions of the crystalline heart vibration, and to provide another access point or platform to the crystalline energies through the heart centre.

The Crystalline Ring

Crystalline light is high-frequency light, and through the previous root races it has gradually been introduced and anchored into the Planet. This seeding process has been slow and at times painful for humanity, as older frequencies have been removed and replaced by the higher crystalline vibrations. At the same time, the dark song of the dark crystal skulls has prevented humanity from claiming its rightful place — in the family of light, and within the true calling of crystalline light. The previous pages of this book outline a number of the crystalline changes that are taking place, and which will come about, as a direct result of the infusion of crystalline light, and in response to the dimensional doorways and probable realities that the crystal skulls will manifest. Humanity is now at a crossroads, and a decision has been made upon which direction to follow — namely, into the light, and the new dawn of love that is calling. The dark is on the defensive, and it is being driven back from humanity's side. For too long the dark frequencies have held sway, as humanity has agonised over its very essence and its connection with Divinity.

The time is fast approaching when all of the past will have changed

for good. The collective vote for the light and the song of light has been
made, and humanity has accepted, at one level, the need to change.
There is still much that must happen in order for this change to take
place, and for the new frequencies being offered as part of the Sixth
Root Race library of light and love to form in human awareness.
However, small groups of light workers have recognised the need to
change time-lines from the Fifth Root Race to the Sixth Root Race, and
the Divine Plan of the Father Meher Baba is in full flow.

Humanity now has to accept, on a deep level, something that was
promised long ago. This promise was forged in crystalline light signified
by a divine crystalline ring, and humanity is now on the point of
accepting this ring as part of the unity of mind and heart with God the
Father. The ring also tells of the new dawn of crystalline light and love
on Earth. It sets an energetic standard for crystalline light that must be
attained before the ring can be fully invoked into matter. This invocation
must be earned, and humanity now stands at the cusp of Divinity, where
the promise of old can be called in.

The promise of the ring was made aeons ago — near the
beginning of Earth's history, and early on in humanity's evolution. The
ring represented for humanity an opportunity to become like the
Divine, and to house and hold within human form, Divine Frequencies
of light and love. The ring symbolised this marriage between Heaven
and Earth.

The formation of the ring arose as part of the seeding of the crystal
skulls into the Planet. The skulls were created first on the inner planes,
and then manifested physically, through a process known as 'the
formation'. The formation is a Divine Seeding-mechanism that captures
the Divine Crystalline Essences of the seventh plane, and calls this into
formation within a matrix of high-frequency light and unconditional
love. This is the love that calls to all in creation, and which is at the root
of creation itself. It is the love that forms the fabric of everything within
and around us. It is the love that binds us all together. Within the
formation, this love is called into the crystalline frequencies, and forms

the underlying frequency of crystalline love. It is the love of the Father as He looks at a reflection of Himself in the Ocean of Divine Bliss.

> In the beginning of the Divine Dawn, when the soft lights and gentle hues become unfurled in an energetic flux of exquisite beauty, the formation of the crystalline matrix of liquid light and love was established by the Father. The blueprint for all of the crystalline frequencies was contained within it.

The formation, then, is the emergence of the crystalline frequencies from the Ocean of Divine Bliss. These are segregated out of the Divine Ocean, and they form a Divine Crystalline Ocean that houses all possible crystalline frequencies.

This crystalline ocean is the birthing point for crystalline energies, and for the subsequent seeding of these frequencies in the higher planes. The Divine Crystalline Ocean is made of liquid crystalline light — it is a wash of crystalline frequencies, within which are the seeds of crystalline light that, on one level, constitute the seeding-mechanism for the formation of the crystal skulls. Because the wash of crystalline frequencies is part of this seeding-mechanism, the formation will always have specific overtonings within it. To access these overtonings will require the peeling off of one layer of reality after another. In a very real sense, this is what the crystalline frequencies and the crystal skulls offer us all — an underlying reality that forms our truth of today, but which will be superseded by a different reality tomorrow. Today's truth becomes tomorrow's obsolescent information, as layer after layer is peeled off during the Divine Play of light and information. Throughout this book, the crystal skull frequencies have been offering different versions of realities, realities that represent different layers that can be peeled off to reveal a deeper level of reality. This play of the Divine is all about going deeper within, and peeling off the layers to access a deeper level of reality, and of Divine Light, Love and Information.

As we peel off these different layers of crystalline information and light, we are offered a different view of what lies beneath. The formation, through its matrix of love in crystalline unity, offers us a different view of crystalline light. The formation, as the seed-bearer and initiator of new crystal frequencies, represents the raw, undiluted crystalline energy within, which is then moulded and formed into different frequencies.

This matrix of crystalline light and love can be developed and amplified in countless different ways. One of its aspects is that it is at once a crystalline liquid, and yet can reflect the patterns of the solid crystalline form. The internal geometry of the liquid crystalline form, and the information contained within the matrix structure, can be replicated in any portions of this crystalline liquid that are separated from the whole matrix. Thus new crystalline energies, or ultimately crystal skulls that are birthed out of the matrix, will hold within them the same internal light and information structure as the whole liquid matrix. They will have their own internal liquid geometry of form, that holds and reflects light. Solid crystals have a similar structure.

The formation describes how crystalline objects and essences are created within this matrix of crystalline light — The Divine Crystalline Ocean. Within the internal geometry of the crystalline liquid there are nodes of light focus, which concentrate the light, and form points of aggregation for more light. As the gravity of light at each of these points builds, they begin to form minute crystal seeds, which then act as the initiators or points around which crystalline light can continue to build. Since these seeds are formed out of the crystalline liquid and its informational matrix, they contain within them an exact replica of all that has been held in the liquid. They are like exact replicas of the crystalline liquid, but are now held and formed in a more concentrated focus of light and energy. This concentration of light is the axis around which the crystal skulls and other crystalline essences ultimately form, depending upon the Intent and Will of the Father as manifested in the Divine Crystalline Ocean. Through the Will of the Father new crystal skulls are formed, and through the Intent of the Father new crystalline beings are born. The Father formed the Divine Crystalline Ring from the Divine Crystalline Ocean in a similar way.

> The Divine Crystalline Ring is a ring of love. It is a ring of crystalline fire and a ring of crystalline light. It is a ring to seal the promise, and a ring to help us hear the call within. It is a ring that forms in the heart, and says that I want to be a part; a part of the new Root Race, and the dawn of humanity into grace. It is the ring that is offered to the light, and the ring that will keep humanity from the night. It is a ring that calls to God, and seals the union of Heaven above and Earth below. It is a ring of love that forms a fire within, and ignites the light to the door within. Love is a burning ring, and it will make your heart sing.

So, the Divine Crystalline Ring is offered to humanity as a recognition of what will have been earned through experience and the formation of the new seeds of love that are now being birthed in heart and soul. This new love now calls to our crystalline hearts within.

The Crystal Heart of the Divine Logos

Within the Heart of God the Beloved, there is a crystalline heart that calls the pulse-beat of all that is in crystalline creation. It represents the pulse-beat of life, and the web of Divine Love that underpins life. This is the Crystalline Heart of the Divine Logos. The frequencies are beyond compare, and they represent within them everything that is crystalline. The Crystalline Heart is the central crystalline focus that carved out the Divine Piano of crystalline notes. As the Father plays the Divine Piano, the Divine Notes originate from the Crystalline Heart, and send out the call to all crystalline life. The Crystalline Heart embodies all the frequencies of love, and within the crystalline notes these frequencies echo the songs of love. The Crystalline Heart comes in many different crystalline guises, and has been played by many Perfect Masters and Avatars, past and present. One of the great players of the Crystalline Heart is the Christos, as the Cosmic Christ sends out His

Divine Love in crystalline form. Both the Father Meher Baba and the Cosmic Christ embody the Crystalline Heart, and call it into matter through the keynotes of crystalline creation. The Crystalline Heart matches the frequencies of all that is in creation, and it is the prime creator of all the crystalline frequencies. It is like 'the everything and the nothing' of the crystalline world.

The frequencies from the Crystalline Heart of the Divine Father are then stepped down into creation through a series of divine filters who match and model the initial highest frequencies, but who, within their own intelligence, present additional layers, so that the frequencies can be received and digested by all other life forms. The first stepping-stone to the Crystalline Heart of the Divine Logos is the crystal heart of the Solar Logos. The Solar Logos represents the Word of God, as manifested in the Son. The Crystalline Heart of the Solar Logos matches that of the Divine Logos, in that it is like a twin: It is a perfect replica, but one that is slightly lower in frequency than the Divine Logos. A similar stepping-down occurs in the Planetary Logos, where the Crystalline Heart is also present, albeit in a slightly diluted form from the Solar Logos. The term 'diluted' is used advisedly here, because the frequencies involved are beyond our capacity to hold, and to earth into the Planet. Within these Crystalline Hearts are held the blueprints for all of crystalline creation, throughout the different spheres.

Ultimately these Crystalline Heart frequencies are stepped down into humanity, and as the Sixth Root Race evolves, and humanity steps into its time-line and love-line, there will be an opportunity to remodel humankind's crystalline heart. The goal for the human race will be to attain these central frequencies of crystalline light as embodied in heart, and for us this ultimate heart frequency will be the Golden Crystalline Heart. This is the Heart of the Christos and the Heart of the Divine, merged in matter and expressed in unity of form. The Golden Heart represents the golden vibration of love that is then housed within a crystalline matrix. The Crystalline Heart has love as its central focus, and embraces a host of crystalline frequencies radiating love. The underpinning frequency for this irradiation is unconditional love, and the Crystalline Heart resonates this frequency to all who are prepared to listen.

The challenge for humanity will be to build a collective vibration that can ascend within the love-lines of the Sixth Root Race, and create a connection with the Golden Crystalline Heart. The pattern of ascendancy will be forged through the new frequencies that will be seeded into the Planet — frequencies which have been described above, and which are primarily embodied in the Divine Banquet.

For many at this point, the first step will be to connect with their own crystalline heart within. As the representation of stepped-down frequencies from the Crystalline Heart of the Divine, it will be important for us to tune into our own heart. There is a real need to feel the Divine pulse-beat of crystalline light within, to soar on the wings of crystalline notes of bliss, to hear the inner calling of the Divine Kiss, and to echo within the silence and purity of the Crystalline Heart. Within a single crystalline note of purity is contained all that is necessary to feel the pulse-beat of the heart within. To first feel this inner crystalline note is to open up to pure light and love. The note can be felt within the heart centre, as the crystalline light builds and unfolds. *Feel* the crystalline light-frequencies ascending and, as the heart centre expands to accommodate them, take time to feel, within this sea of crystalline light, the inner pulse-beat. It will be at once like the pure stillness of the crystalline ocean within, yet behind this there will be a pulse of pure love, a pulse of crystalline light that is calling forth. As you feel this pulse-beat, allow the heart to listen, and to invoke it.

As the energies and the new high-frequency crystalline notes of the Sixth Root Race are downloaded into our systems, this pulse-beat of the Crystalline Heart will begin to change. Firstly, as we build our crystalline light bodies, the focus of the pulse-beat will become clearer, and it will spread from the heart to all that is crystalline within us: thus our crystalline light body will pulse in unison with the inner heartbeat. Then, as we build the connection with our inner crystalline essence, the pulse-beat will become stronger, singing a more insistent song. As we connect and merge with other crystalline songs through the crystal skulls, we shall begin to hear other pulse-beats. At first these may appear to dance to a different rhythm within, but with time we shall come to recognise that within there is a similar pulse-beat of crystalline love. There may be variations in the song, but the underlying theme will always be crystalline love.

The infusion of Divine Light from the Cosmic Christ into the crystalline grid surrounding the Planet and connecting all its life forms, will open us up to a deeper pulse-beat of love from the Crystalline Heart. We shall begin to sense a golden tinge to our crystalline heart, and to feel a deeper love connection with the pulse-beat and the crystalline song. Our crystalline hearts will be transformed and will sing the joy of true crystalline love. As Divine Frequency after Divine Frequency is systematically downloaded into humanity as part of the Sixth Root Race medley, the crystalline heart within humanity will become more collective, and will forge a group consciousness bound in love and light. As life after life passes in matter, the crystalline hearts of those dancing the Sixth Root Race song, will build a Crystalline Heart of exquisite purity and clarity. The hearts of those in matter and working with the light will build unity through love, and diversity through life's frequencies, while all the time feeling the ascendancy of the Crystalline Heart.

Lifetime after lifetime will see the Crystalline Heart become more golden, as specks of golden light are collected in It. Each speck will represent new love frequencies as they are gathered-in through experience in matter. Love after love, life after life, will forge an array of more and more refined love frequencies, which will touch the heart in so many ways, opening it and peeling back layer after layer. The love frequencies will become finer and finer, to the point where it would seem impossible for the vibrations to embody love in yet another way: and yet they will, as the songs of the heart play new notes, and the Crystalline Heart unfurls love frequency after love frequency.

Ultimately there will come a point when love is felt and seen in everything, where love is the underlying fabric of all, and where the heart is truly known as the initiator of all crystalline light. Crystalline love will melt within, being felt at deeper and deeper levels, to the point where it will seem that no more love can be encompassed. But still love will call, holding the Divine Harmonic within its thrall, with the Crystalline Heart blessed in bliss, and surrounded by love's all. Octave after octave of love's sweet kiss will flow through the crystalline hearts, calling in more and more light, held in the Divine's embrace. Love will be in the all.

Ultimately, those who have heard the call of love, and forged a bridge with the unity and love within; and heard the calls of the Divine Father, the Cosmic Christ and others; these will have earned the right to hold and become the Golden Crystalline Heart. Their golden hearts will sing out the true crystalline song, and they will embody all the crystalline frequencies within and without. The Golden Crystalline Heart will then truly be within humanity. When these changes have taken place in the few, and have then been passed on to the many, then the promise of the past, of a new crystalline light on Earth will have been honoured.

Crystalline Balance

As the wash of new crystalline frequencies is seeded into heart and third eye, there will come a time when an attunement between heart and third eye takes place. In the introduction, a new emerging connection between heart and third eye was hinted at, where the two could interchange with each other, or merge to become one. With the ascendancy of higher crystalline light into our space, the ability to see and feel the new crystalline vibrations will intensify. The crystal skulls will help to forge bridges of the heart to the Crystalline Heart of the Divine, while the informational superhighways of crystalline light will connect us with the new planetary, solar system and galactic crystalline grids. With all that is held in heart and third eye, the Sixth Root Race re-alignment will begin to forge new telepathic links between light workers, as soul begins to merge with soul.

The balance of the head versus the heart will also dramatically shift within planet Earth, which has a 50/50 balance between the two. The new crystalline energies will look to re-focus this balance, while maintaining the same percentages in heart and mind. The aim will be to dig deeper into the heart, to mine new crystalline frequencies, and also to re-arrange and re-align the mental focus of the head. Crystalline light is mental light, and the new crystalline frequencies will demand that this be housed in our brains, replacing the slow-frequency astral light that has fed the mind for so long. Mental light, as high-frequency light, will first burn our minds and cleanse our mental focus. As the mind is stripped away and re-focused with mental light, and as our hearts are re-structured to accommodate high-frequency crystalline light, there will be a major opportunity to bring the two together. Love of the heart will be merged with mental informational matrices of light, so that the balance between love and informational light can be maintained.

In order for this to take place, the heart centre will need to migrate upwards to the third eye, and to fuse with the frequencies held within it. This fusion will bring through a new understanding of mental light, where this can be housed in love, and understood through a dialogue with the heart. Similarly, the heart will enjoy the high-frequency mental input, and new information that will enable it to open up even more. The internal space of both heart and third eye will need to expand significantly, so that one can merge with the other.

As this merging pattern builds, it will also be possible, for brief periods, to house, the third eye energy within the heart centre. It will be like using the heart centre as a tuning-fork for what is received through the third eye. The movement will allow a new point of appraisal of new in-coming frequencies, while at the same time allowing a point of balance and centeredness to emerge as a whole.

Ultimately the heart will move up into the third eye space on a more permanent basis, so that we shall be able to see with our hearts in a true and complete way. This type of 'seeing' will be very different from what is experienced now, for within **this** seeing will be the Crystalline Heart of love, and the purity and unity of crystalline consciousness. All will be held in balance, as the higher crystalline frequencies build up the internal spaces of both heart and third eye. As time goes by, the hearts and third eyes of Sixth Root Race light workers will be able to span vast galaxies of frequencies, to attune these to the heart within, and to reflect and balance the higher love frequencies that need to be earthed into the Planet. In effect, this balancing between heart and third eye will allow everything to be connected to through a divine filter of love.

The other main shift in this crystalline balancing will concern the space that will have been vacated in the heart centre: for where previously there was a pattern of crystalline heart energy, there will be an empty space. This space will offer an opportunity for light workers to enter a new and much deeper pattern of energy: it will allow new doorways to be opened to the silence within, to a place where there is nothing, and where in the silence a true balance can begin to be established. Meher Baba used to say that in true silence is real work done. So in the silence of the heart can new inner depths and connections be forged with the Divine. The opportunities for this new opening will be limitless. In the silence, true merging with God can take place.

The space within the heart centre will allow new energies — immense Divine Presences — to grace our planet. For those light workers who succeed in building this new alignment and crystalline balance, the heart centre will represent another grand opening. Divine Beings such as Perfect Masters, and other Avataric frequencies from the past, will be able to connect with these new crystalline systems, and infuse the Planet with a vast array of Divine Frequencies. New patterns of light from multiple Perfect Masters will allow a host of new frequencies to be brought through in a new and direct manner. Other high-frequency energies from the higher mental planes will be given greater access to the Planet, and those on the seventh plane will be able to direct their energies into Earth in a totally new way. The effect of all this will be to drive Earth's frequency-vibration upwards, and to allow a new level of Divine Frequencies to be manifested in physical matter. Within the space and silence of the heart, new formats for earthing these Frequencies will be explored, as the new frequency-holders of crystalline light become the new living librarians of Divine Love. These individuals will have energetic systems without parallel, as they will be able to invoke and contain within their systems a massive array of different beings and frequencies.

The space within will also offer new inner pathways to God. Humanity will continue in earnest with the pathway set out in the evolution and involution of consciousness. As soul aspects come towards the completion of their reincarnatory programme, and ascend up into the seventh plane to become God-realised, and succeed in bringing their systems into crystalline balance within, the opportunity for using the space within to undertake the First Divine Journey may become possible, and thereafter, the Second and Third Divine Journeys.

The First, Second and Third Divine Journeys are usually undertaken in physical matter by those on the path to becoming Perfect Masters. However, the new frequencies within the Planet will allow a different pattern of Perfect Mastery to emerge. This new pattern will seek to bring through an even higher array of Divine frequency-notes than before, and to house them differently within the physical systems of those few on this path. In the First Divine Journey, the God-realised soul has to pass through eternal bliss. The majority of souls remain in this state. However, the few souls that do complete the First Divine Journey, can progress further. On the Second and Third Divine Journeys, the God-realised soul must first merge more deeply into God, and then bring back down into matter the frequencies of the seventh plane. A further journey back down through the planes is necessary, so that these new unconditional frequencies can be anchored all the way from the seventh to the zero planes, and held within the system of the emerging Perfect Master. The new pattern of energy system being developed within the Sixth Root Race will allow for this process to be carried out in a different way, and for all of these frequencies to be contained within the heart centre as well as the third eye.

In the Sixth Root Race, our energetic systems will undergo a massive shift. The old chakra system will be totally re-structured to hold the new crystalline frequencies, and a new dynamic between heart and third eye will allow new dimensional spaces to be created inside us. The scope and beauty of this new crystalline energetic system will be truly astounding, and humanity's ascendancy into new time-lines and love-lines will ensure that the Planet enters a period of crystalline light and love blessed by the Father. The calling of the Crystalline Heart, and the love within, will echo out across planet Earth, the solar systems, the galaxies, and beyond, fuelling new highways of light and stellar crystalline pathways.

Humanity's frequency will continue to ascend throughout the evolution of the Sixth Root Race, as crystalline frequencies merge and meld, as crystalline hearts commune in Divine Love and as the crystal skulls sing new songs of crystalline light and love. The emergence of the true crystalline race in humanity will echo what was promised many ages ago and will reflect a pattern of crystalline form that was developed in ages past. As our frequencies continuously ascend, we will become like living crystal skulls, our centres merging as one with the crystal skull frequencies. Our systems will become physical doorways of crystalline light, which they will radiate to all around. Our physical body shape will also alter, to reflect the new crystalline patterns within bone, tissue and fluids; our physical systems will become much purer, and will be strengthened to hold the new light-frequencies.

Ultimately, the astral light that is being processed will be cleared, and there will be a much more direct connection between the mental and the physical planes: the filtering of mental light through astral light will no longer be necessary, since our physical vehicles will be able to capture and digest mental light frequencies directly. Consequently, the seeding of new frequencies and informational matrices into humanity will be much more direct. Humanity's new status in terms of frequency and light will be seen in the crystalline centres of those representing the Sixth Root Race. The crystalline hearts of all who are forging the new destiny of the Sixth Root Race will sing the song of true crystalline light, and will hear the keynotes of the Divine Father as He plays out the melodies and symphonies on the Divine Crystalline Piano. The Father's performance will be like no other: it will command a standing ovation from all life, both outer and inner.

In conclusion, then, the crystal skulls and the new pattern of crystalline frequencies represent massive keys to our inner doorways of light and love. As through intent and will we ascend these new crystalline frequencies, and begin to earth them within ourselves, our lives will be transformed. The purity of crystalline light will be revealed to us, and the song of the crystal skulls will call to us in our everyday lives, in our dreams, and in the inner recesses of our subconscious. Wave after wave of new, high-frequency crystalline light will bombard our systems, and the choice will be ours: whether or not to grasp these new opportunities with both hands? In one sense it is easy to wake up to this signal within, and to recognise the love contained within a single splinter of crystalline light — let alone, the massive frequency amplifiers that are the crystal skulls, whose very depth, illumination and brilliance of light are beyond description. What is perhaps harder, after this recognition and activation, is the decision over what to do about it.

While it is possible to be open to the new crystalline frequencies, and to allow them to simply wash through our systems, it is also possible for communication with them to become one of being, and one of action through intent.

We do have a choice about whether to be passive or active within this new wash of Divine Frequencies. Remaining passive means just that: letting the frequencies flow through, and allowing one's focus to remain diffuse and non-directed. In contrast, to become activate means to apply will and intent, aligning that will and intent with the wishes of the Divine Father, and working actively with the new frequencies, according to the Divine Plan. There are opportunities for all of us within this unfolding play, each of them unique, and there is no competition within this context: only a recognition that as God's light-sparks, we have the opportunity to be of service in specific, weird and wonderful ways, and to acknowledge the flow of energy in heart and third eye, allowing the invocation from within to mould the reality without. Nothing is ever as it seems, and as the diverse flux of crystalline energies is seeded into our planet, the awesome opportunities for opening up within are limitless.

The spread of new crystalline frequencies entering the Planet has been ordained and the key issue is what we do with them. A programme to banish fear, remove slow frequency disinformation and clear the Planet of old root race frequencies is well underway, so that the scene is set for humanity to ascend to the new frequencies that have been prepared. These ascending changes will first manifest in the few and then in the many, as part of the new Divine Hologram of Light.

All that is needed on our part is commitment, right use of will, and the emotional desire to manifest into our consciousness the changes that have been foretold. The choices are there; and there are many higher-plane guides waiting and hoping to be of assistance to those who choose to pursue a more active path into the light. Similarly, on the inner planes there are many crystal skulls waiting to be accessed and activated as part of the emerging consciousness of multi-dimensional reality.

Ultimately, it will be the focus, will and intent of humanity that will determine the success of the Sixth Root Race experiment. Earth is on an ever-upward spiral of hosting new frequencies, and the more humanity invokes and expresses these higher frequencies, then the greater the success of the experiment. There is no limit to what we can house within our systems, nor to how we can access and bring through our divinity as part of the Father's Plan. With each successive shift in frequency, we shall gain a clearer picture of what we truly are, and what we are destined to become. There will be many obstacles and abysses to be overcome, but this all represents part of the Divine Game. The beauty, heartfelt love and unity in all will be a beacon to us as we ascend our own crystalline mountains of light, acknowledging that we are all part of the Divine Crystalline Ocean of light and love within.

In bringing to a close this description of the pattern of frequencies embodied in the crystal skull vibrations, I should like to offer a few short channellings that contain some of their keynotes, and which formed part of a recognition in myself of what the crystal skulls have to offer (these are but one interpretation). There are three separate channellings in all; the third was received just before the start of the year 2000.

Crystal Skull Channelling 1

All is connection. All that unfoldeth is about connection and communication. We represent the skull frequencies that are empowering your planet at this time. The multitude of connections, planes, is becoming manifest to a select few of you. This is as it should be. As crystalline entities of Divine origin, we salute and recognise your status, both on the inner and outer planes. Through merging with us and among yourselves, you will begin to generate and access a new diversity of crystalline skull frequencies that has yet to be presented within the physical planes on this planet. We seek to seed these frequencies within you, and to transmit them using you as frequency-carriers, to carry this beyond you, to those that seek and search, and that know deep down how to unite. We do not seek any recompense, in energetic or other terms. This is our contract, our work, and our duty and our destiny. We can combine a huge array of frequencies for downloading into you. All that you need is stability, strength, openness of purpose and clarity of mind, and single-mindedness of heart: a single-mindedness that is dedicated to the Divine Father, the One who oversees and sees beyond all. The One who is the beginning and the end; the Evermore, throughout all that is known and unknown. We seek to bring through the truth, the harmony, the destiny, the clarity and the clarion call of His

Divine Frequencies, and it is through our unique crystalline rapport with you and the Divine Father that we wish so much to amplify and expand at present.

The crystalline energy that we manifest and symbolise, represents an applied focus of will, and shall at first be stepped down for your matrix of energies to hold and contain. It is an appliance of light in matter, guided through our love, understanding and expertise within the crystalline spheres. We span all the planes, beyond the planes and within the planes. This you should know and understand with all your heart. For true crystallinity is at the centre of all things, it is of all things, and it is this emergence, or re-emergence, that is the key to the crystal skull frequencies at this time. You both have a strong recognition and rapport with us, and we shall not bore you with the details of this from the past, for it is the present, the now, that matters, and upon the future with which we wish to focus. You may select and draw down any of our crystal skull frequencies as you wish, either through the physical amplifiers that are present on the Planet, or through the etheric, astral, mental amplifiers that can be accessed within your internal consciousness. This is simple, yet profound, and should not be treated lightly, for in truth the light that we emit, that we are, goes beyond all your imaginings, and all that is known and unknown to you. This you should comprehend, respect and complement with your developing frequencies; for from now, all is change in the Divine Emergence of the new root race frequencies, and in the merging of your higher and lower self or vehicles, for we will be one as ever and always with you.

We seek to connect and infuse these light frequencies within you, within an orchestrated pattern of remedial work, focusing on each of your chakra systems as appropriate. You may focus on any or all of the crystal skull vibrations that are known and unknown to you, through simply calling us in as the skull vibrations, and accessing the highest vibrations. This is simple, and as I have asserted, profound. Feel through the eyes, through the crown, into the liquid light elixir of crystalline divinity that we embody, represent, manifest and make plain within all the spheres. As you feel the Divine Love of the Divine Father Meher Baba, feel through to His Heart, to His Light, to His utter and complete Divinity. For it is His Word, His Thoughts, His Manifestation and Guidance that come through us to you, and are within us through His Grace. So feel these frequencies, and feel the Divine Love, the Divine Knowledge and the Divine Understanding as you stand at the doorway of Divine Illumination and Grace. Feel the freedom, feel the blessing and the understanding that the Divine Father has for you. Feel His Love, which is beyond all loves, and encompasses all loves. He simply is. So focus. *Feel*.

We will leave you now, and connect again in the immediacy of the Divine Flame. With our love.

Crystal Skull Channelling 2

Connection. All is connection. The mysteries of Divine Intelligence and of the Universe are based entirely upon the crystalline connection that operates multi-dimensionally. *Feel* into this connection. Feel the vibration. Feel the heart. Feel the source; and merge, merge, and merge. We of the crystal skull vibrations greet you and send our love, and ask for you to remember and connect with us at all times. The crystalline vibrations of Seclusion Hill represent the doorway, the key, to the true Sixth Root Race and dimensional emergence at this time. Feel into this vibration, this key, this doorway, for it is that which will truly align you with all Sixth Root Race vibrations as they are entering the Planet now. The force, the beauty, the rhythm of this vibration are indeed evident and all around: and yet the unity of its crystalline array has yet to be fully comprehended on the physical planes.

You, as you recognise, are a torch-bearer, a seeder, a seed of hearts and minds, of those around you, and those way beyond you, of whom you have no physical-plane recognition, but with whom you have contracts and debts owed on other levels. All of this will come to pass as your true crystalline divinity begins to take shape even more clearly than it is at present. You may ask how to become more crystalline, how to merge more with crystalline energies, when you feel you may have connected at a deep enough level already. The answer is simple — to merge and merge, and merge again, for the unfolding of the crystalline frequencies knows no bounds, no limits, and is clear for you to connect with. It goes on and on. So as you merge in the liquid light of the Divine Infusion of the Father's Crystalline Nature, it is truly that you are finding the door, the key, to merging with the Divine Father.

This multiplicity of frequencies, these scatterings and bringings back and forth of the fragmentation of the subtle and physical plane levels within your being, are also part of the true crystalline nature of everything. For it is true that in crystallinity you can be in one place and at other places at once. As you merge with the crystal you are everywhere, within the crystal and beyond it. And as you are with one crystal, so it is that you can be connected to yet another, and another and another. The possibilities are truly limitless and exponential in their intensity and awesomeness.

So by merging with your true crystalline nature, and taking that nature, and merging it with the Divine Infusion of the Father, and bringing forth frequencies of His Will, His Heart and His Mind, it is true that you can reach greater and greater depths of unity and uniformity. The Sixth Root Race vibration, or sequences of vibrations, although you can liken it to a scale in music, is infinitely more than this. For on each single scale, there are multiplicities of resonances, frequencies, overtones, undertones and re-chargings that go beyond the physical and other plane-levels associated with each of those frequencies. The crystal skull formation, or the seeding of the crystal skull formations within this array of dimensional frequencies, is particularly important, and can only be clearly understood through merging and melding with the true skull frequencies.

As you stand with the crystal skulls arrayed around you, within your mind's eye, it is true that you should merge with as many as possible, as well as each separately, individually and yet collectively, in an overlay of frequencies. This will be facilitated by your true crystalline nature. But practice and connect; for as you merge, you will feel how the crystalline nature has been calling to you over the aeons: which is a unity, it is a oneness; and it is simply everywhere.

We salute your endeavours and commitment, and feel within your hands the presence of a crystal skull upon your lap. Feel yourself merge with this vibration, and allow it to connect with each of your centres, starting with the merging of your skull with that of the crystal skull. And as it rotates and merges and connects, feel the Divine Fire within your third eye re-awaken. Feel the streams of energy running through your head, and then feel the remainder of your body becoming crystalline; a uniformity and a merging. On each hand is placed a series of crystal skull rings, a reminder of who and what you are, and within your heart feel the essence of what could be termed a Master Skull — the major key. Feel these frequencies unfurl and resonate within your inner space. And as these streams of light unify and unite you with our frequencies and with those of the Divine Father, acknowledge form this day henceforth, that you are truly one with our vibration. Your channelling, your painting, will be amplified many times over. A dawn, within a dawn, within a dawn.

Message for the New Millennium

While it is true that time is but an illusion, and that this transition into the next century is but a passing through another doorway, we of the crystal skull vibrations wish to send our Divine Love and Light at this time. The new vortices of energy that are opening at this time represent great changes, great challenges and great hopes and aspirations. The doorways that have been opened to access the new frequencies of this New Age have only just begun, and there is more, much more, which awaits you all in the transformation into the next root race.

A key, if you like, is the breadth and scope of all of these frequencies. While we represent a particular light-stream of crystalline frequencies (although we use that word advisedly, since "stream" can mean many things, and in this context is not intended to be limiting, but rather universal), we represent a resonant point of access to the Divine Father. Our spectrum covers all the planes, and countless universes, and it is at this point open to you to choose where within our spectrum you focus. We shall be waiting, we shall be there to greet you, and we shall be open to providing access to a whole new range of crystalline frequencies of liquid light and love. All that matters is the intent. Bring us into your hearts with love, with steadfastness of purpose, and with quietness of mind and heart, and allow our frequencies to spread throughout your body, through every fibre, until you can "hold" no more. Merge with us, and allow the alignment of new energies to open new doorways within you, and to allow the ancient doorways of distrust to be closed forever.

Glossary

Astral Levels

The astral levels represent a series of light frequencies that house a variety of different energies; predominant among them, emotions. The astral levels are a more subtle level of energy than the physical. They are split into three main tiers — lower, middle and higher, each of which houses different levels of astral light. The lower astral is slow-frequency, and carries within it all of the grosser emotions and energies, while the middle astral captures a higher frequency level, and is where humanity tends to anchor its inner awareness. The higher astral levels carry a higher frequency light, and embody higher attributes and emotions. Astral light dominates the lower plane levels i.e. the first, second and third planes, although it is found in lower percentage levels in the fifth and sixth planes. As of May 2003, the astral levels became totally opened up to humanity.

Chakras

Chakras are energy centres housed at specific points in the body, and function as dimensional doorways between its different energy systems. The outer physical manifestation of a chakra has a representation within, which corresponds to the chakra system of the subtle anatomy. Thus chakras act as doorways between the physical, etheric, astral and beyond. There are seven main chakra centres in the body, plus a series of secondary chakra points, such as those in the soles of the feet, the palms of the hands, and at bone joints. The seven main centres are the base (or root), the hara (or sexual), the solar plexus, the heart, the throat, the third eye and the crown. This book focuses mainly on the heart chakra, which houses series of different love frequencies; and the third eye, which is associated with seeing 'within'.

Crystalline Frequencies

Crystalline frequencies are higher light energies that are sourced from the crystalline realms in the higher planes, particularly from the fifth, sixth and seventh planes. Crystalline light contains a specific frequency bandwidth possessing an internal geometry which defines its crystalline nature. Like physical crystals on Earth, and throughout the Universe, crystalline frequencies irradiate a pattern of light that is defined by the internal structure of the crystal. Crystalline frequencies can arise in a number of different forms, all of which express crystalline light; these include the crystal skulls, and crystalline guides and intelligences in the higher planes.

Crystal Skulls

The crystal skulls are beacons of Divine Light, and are irradiators of crystalline light sourced directly from God. The crystal skull, at its highest and purest level, is a Divine amplifier, a Divine creator of reality, a beacon of Divine Light, and a pattern of reality as manifest through the Divine Father's Will and Intent. The true frequency embodied by the crystal skulls is therefore one of unconditional love presented within a crystalline format. Crystal skulls can be accessed through those found in the physical planes, such as the Mitchell-Hedges crystal skull, or within, through the mental planes. A crystal skull will house within it all the frequencies necessary to define a possible reality, and so working with specific ones will invoke this multi-dimensional aspect of probable realities.

Devas

Devas are alternative life forms that form the underlying matrix to our physical systems, and those of the mineral, animal and plant kingdoms. They are like the glue or life substance that holds everything together at a cellular level. The Devas' awareness is very different from our own, and is focused on feeling: Devas develop and grow through feeling rather than through the power of conscious thought. In humans, Devas can be visualised as having a rat-like appearance. The colouration of the fur and size of whiskers will indicate the frequency level that the Deva is operating at. For example, if the fur is seen as grey or brown, then this will represent a lower frequency than, say, white fur. The new energies that will be born through Sixth Root Race evolution will push up the frequency of the Devas in a stunning manner.

Dimensional Doorways

Dimensional doorways are gates or portals from one dimension to another. They can be doorways through time and space, and can connect with different levels on the inner planes. For example, the heart and third eye centres are dimensional doorways into the different plane levels. Dimensional doorways come in many different shapes, sizes, textures and forms, and can be accessed in a variety of ways. A number of doorways have been set up to give access to Earth through the 'ring-pass-not', the band of blue light encircling the Earth, that acts as a barrier to the free movement of energy and information to the Planet. Incarnating souls must pass through the 'ring-pass-not', and lose all past-life memories in the process.

Divine Journeys

Souls have the opportunity to undertake a number of Divine Journeys as part of their evolution, once they have become God-realised. All incarnating souls will go through, on average, 8,400,000 lives before becoming God-realised. The First Divine Journey is the soul's journey after God-realisation through what is termed Divine Bliss. The soul may enter subsequent Divine Journeys, depending upon the trajectory mapped out through the seventh plane. Generally speaking, only those souls destined to become Perfect Masters undergo the Second and Third Divine Journeys. If in the First Divine Journey the soul merges back into God, then in the Second Divine Journey, which happens in timelessness, the soul becomes God, living His own infinite Life, becoming the very Source of Infinite Knowledge, Bliss and Existence. The soul becomes completely identified with God. In the Third Divine Journey, it then travels back down through all of the planes, to become simultaneously God-conscious and human-conscious.

Divine Ocean of Bliss

The Divine Ocean is the Source, or the formation of God. When the soul is at the Source, within God, it is part of the 'Divine Ocean' that is the unity of everything. Within the Divine Ocean there occurs an ongoing process of vibrationary changes that whip up the atmosphere. This atmosphere, the Breath of the Creator, separates off from the Ocean small droplets of divinity.

Dragon Light

Dragon light is high-frequency light that embodies dragon energy. This represents a higher vehicle of expression, one that manifested early on in the creation of life by the Father. One of our highest forms of expression is as dragons, and we now have the opportunity to connect with these much older aspects of ourselves, which are expressed as dragons with wings, claws, long necks, and different skin colours that reflect the age of the dragon and its status.

Evolution/Involution

Evolution refers to the progressive evolution of consciousness from the stone stage, through the plant and animal kingdoms, culminating in the human form. The history of evolution is the gradual development of consciousness.

Involution refers to the process whereby the consciousness of the soul gradually disengages from the physical or gross world, and turns inward. During the first six planes, the soul gradually withdraws the focus of its consciousness from the gross sphere to the subtle sphere, and thence to the mental sphere (see also Planes of Consciousness). At the seventh plane the soul experiences Realisation, and knows itself to be God. More detailed information can be found in *God Speaks* by Meher Baba.

Frequencies

Frequencies are the vibratory notes or signals that are held by all bodies, both animate and inanimate. They can vibrate across a whole vibratory spectrum, from high to low, and will span the physical, etheric, astral and mental levels. A slow frequency note can be represented by emotions such as fear, anger, or depression;

such energies often stem from old disharmonies and in many cases are negatively charged. Higher frequency vibrations may be represented by emotions such as joy, and feelings of harmony. Frequencies can be presented in multiple ways at the different levels, and mental frequencies will feel very different from, say, astral frequencies.

God-realisation

God-realisation is when the soul experiences itself as God. It is a unique state of consciousness because it is not dependent upon the individual mind, personality, or any other medium. Achieving God-realisation requires the perfect balancing of all karma, both light and dark, and the collection of the totality of experience of matter. It also requires the emancipation of consciousness from the limitations of mind. There are always fifty-six God-realised beings in matter in the world at any one time, and they are always One in consciousness.

Guides

A guide is a source of human energy external to the human personality. It is also an intelligence that communicates with individuals in the physical realms, and generally assists them in following a path that is in their best interests. Guides come in many shapes and forms, and can work etherically, astrally, mentally, or sometimes on a soul level. There are many different types of guide, and the appearance or form of the guide will be a reflection of the plane level at which it is operating. For example, in the lower planes, guides tend to manifest in a more protective aspect, such as soldiers *e.g.* Roman soldiers. Native American Indian guides frequent the middle plane levels, especially the fourth plane, while higher mental guides can appear in a range of different forms, from Chinese to extra-terrestrial. With the transformation into the Sixth Root Race, new levels of guidance are becoming available, including seventh plane guidance.

Higher and Lower Self

Higher and lower self are different expressions of our vehicles of consciousness. The lower self is the physical vehicle in matter. It has its awareness limited through karma, its principal focus on the physical life currently in play in progress. The lower self is the 'younger' self. In contrast, the higher self is the higher vehicle of consciousness: the older self. This operates at the soul level, and is aware of the totality of the soul's expression and experience, and of the overall plan of activity at all levels. As the Sixth Root Race gets underway, there will be a need for many people to build a deeper connection between the higher and the lower self, to create a clear, uninterrupted flow of information between the two.

Love-Lines

Love-lines are inter-dimensional frequencies that operate by using love as a focal point. They reflect different frequencies from different sources, including the Avatar, the Perfect Masters and other life forms, be they human, animal, plant, mineral or extra-terrestrial. Love-lines are lines of energy that will flow from individual to individual through different plane levels, and which can also connect other living energies. The highest-frequency love-lines are those that embody unconditional love: love in its supreme expression. As the Sixth Root Race begins to form, more and more love-lines are being invoked and brought into reality.

Masts

Masts are God-intoxicated souls. Their focus is within and on God and their love of God. Consequently, they have no focus on outside stimuli.

Mental Levels

The mental levels represent the higher frequency levels where mental light is focused. As with the astral levels, there are three main divisions — lower, middle and higher. The mental frequencies are much higher than the astral frequencies, and they embody mental energies. Mental light is typically focused in the higher planes — the fifth and sixth planes. It is also the main frequency within which the crystal skulls can be accessed.

Over-Soul

The Over-Soul is the supreme, universal Soul — Almighty God

— that hosts and leads to the formation of individual souls. It marks a different and deeper expression of God than the soul. It is the next level within God from the soul level. While individual souls are separated from God, the Over-Soul is an expression of God, manifested in the reality of the seventh plane. The Over-Soul hosts all souls, so that individual souls are connected to the Over-Soul by lines of soul energy.

Perfect Masters

A Perfect Master is a God-realised soul who retains God-consciousness and creation-consciousness simultaneously, and who works within creation to help souls towards the realisation of God. The Perfect Master consciously experiences not only infinite knowledge, but also infinite power, infinite bliss, and all goodness. A Perfect Master is one who not only becomes God, but who, after achieving God-realisation, also comes down to the ordinary normal consciousness of humanity (see also Divine Journeys). He or She possesses simultaneously God-consciousness and mental, subtle and gross consciousness. There are five Perfect Masters in physical matter at any one time, three of whom work directly with humanity and two who do not. The five Perfect Masters are part of the fifty-six God-realised beings. Perhaps the best-known recent Perfect Masters were the Perfect Ones who worked directly with Meher Baba, and who were responsible for calling Him down to the Planet. These were Sai Baba of Shirdi, Upasni Maharaj, Tajuddin Baba, Hasrat Babajan and Narayan Maharaj.

Planes of Consciousness

The planes of consciousness, which are also known as the planes of involution of consciousness, are the states of consciousness experienced by the soul while traversing the spiritual path. Another name for them is the 'inner planes'. There are seven main planes, numbered from 1 to 7 in ascending order; and an additional plane, known as the zero plane, lies below the first plane. This represents the point of entry into physical matter for the soul aspect, being the level where it undergoes incarnation first into mineral, then plant and animal form. The zero plane also includes recently-incarnated human beings. Once they have acquired sufficient experience, souls pass through the zero plane into the first plane, and then slowly traverse the other six before becoming God-realised on the seventh. Within each plane there are millions of sub-planes.

During the first six planes, the soul gradually withdraws the focus of its consciousness from the denser gross sphere (the physical) to the finer subtle sphere (the astral), and thence to the even finer mental sphere. As mentioned earlier in the Glossary, this process is known as involution. The subtle sphere consists of the first four planes of consciousness (i.e. the first, second, third and fourth planes) as experienced by the subtle (or astral) body through its subtle impressions. The fourth plane serves as the threshold to the mental spheres (the fifth and sixth planes), but is neither fully subtle nor fully mental. The mental sphere is then experienced by the mental body through its mental impressions. At the seventh plane, the soul experiences Realisation, and knows itself to be God.

Progression up through the planes is accompanied by different levels of light, including astral and mental light. The inner space and energy vibrations of the planes also increase significantly from the zero plane through to the seventh plane.

Reincarnation

A soul aspect entering the physical plane must work its way through all the permutations of matter, through the mineral kingdom, and then the plant and animal kingdoms. It will eventually incarnate in human form, and will then, on average, require 8,400,000 lives to explore the physical realms and to work its way up through the main planes to the seventh plane. On average, each plane will require at least 1 million lives to complete, and sometimes many more. This process of birth and re-birth is known as reincarnation.

Root Races

The root races represent major permutations or cycles of energy within form that have been present on Earth. A root race will have a particular focus in terms of energy, body form, chakra alignment, and arrangement of physical, etheric, astral, and mental bodies. The beginning of each root race has coincided usually with major changes on the Planet, and the destruction of the form of the previous root race. There have been five root races to date — the Adamic, the Hyperborean, the Lemurian, the Atlantean and the Aryan. We are now entering the Sixth Root Race, and this transition from the Fifth Root Race is unique, in that body form is being retained and modified during this evolutionary process.

Shamanistic Robes

A shamanistic robe is a protective frequency note that is invoked through will and intent. Shamanistic robes are used in energy practice: they involve the visualisation of energy structures that surround the aura and seal off one's inner space from any unwanted external frequencies, in both the physical and the inner planes. As thought-forms, shamanistic robes can be invoked in a variety of different ways, depending upon the plane setting and the type of energy work that is to be undertaken. By virtue of their inherent frequency, shamanistic robes also help one to connect with a particular plane level. Typical shamanistic robes include buffalo, owls, wolves and bears.

Soul

A soul is created by the separation of one drop from the Divine Ocean. It then begins a process of becoming aware of itself as being separate from the Source. Most souls, as they begin their downward journey into different realities, split themselves into seven main aspects, with each aspect then splitting into two, thus providing the soul with the capacity to acquire as much information as possible. Soul aspects have the same vibratory structure within the genetic background of the soul. The soul's full cycle is for all of its aspects to separate from the Source, which is timeless; to work its way down from the seventh plane through the planes of consciousness into physical form in the zero plane; and then to work its way back up through the planes for Divine union at the seventh plane. The focus of all souls and soul aspects is to obtain experience in matter, which in turn drives the reincarnatory programme. There are usually only five soul aspects in matter at any one time, and meetings in human form between these aspects represent a true meeting of soul-mates. Such meetings are rare.

Star Children

The star children are older souls who are incarnating into the Planet. They have a strong association with more extra-terrestrial frequencies based upon experience with other stars and planetary systems, and a have a deep reservoir of knowledge. It is this knowledge and understanding which they are keen to gift to humanity.

Supramental Levels

The supramental levels refer to those plane levels above the mental planes i.e to the seventh plane and beyond.

The Avatar

The Avatar is the total manifestation of God in human form on Earth, as the Eternal Living Perfect Master. The Avatar was the first individual soul to emerge from the evolutionary and involutionary process as the Perfect Master, and He is the only One who has ever manifested, or will ever manifest. The Avatar incarnates either every 700 years or every 1400 years, being called into physicality by the five Perfect Masters present on Earth at that time. Whenever the Avatar manifests on Earth, His Godhood gives a universal push, and the result is universal. The Avatar will go by different names, depending on the time period that He is called into incarnation. Meher Baba is the most recent Avatar: He lived from 1894 to 1969. Others have included the Lord Jesus, the Buddha and Zoroaster. The appearance of the Avatar will always signify a big shift in Earth history, as new divine frequencies are fed into all life forms. His appearance always coincides with the spiritual regeneration of humanity. We are currently in an Avataric period, which lasts for 100 years after the Avatar drops His Physical Form.

The Paramatma

The Paramatma is The Supreme Self, The Absolute, The Supreme Divine Being. Paramatman Light is the Light of the Paramatma.

The Wheel of Life

The Wheel of Life represents all the planets in the Universe that are host to the human form. 18,000 of them support human life, and these are arranged around the planet Earth, which is at the centre. Evolving souls will incarnate in these other "Earths", and as they gain experience they will work their way through them until eventually arriving on Earth. In this set-up, Earth represents a finishing school for souls.

Time-Lines

Time-lines are inter-dimensional frequencies that operate within a particular time period. They exist physically, astrally and mentally. Such time periods can be past, present or future, and for an individual soul aspect will be held in place by karma. So a soul aspect can incarnate within a particular time-line to work through its karma. Although time only exists linearly within a physical framework, it is possible for an individual to work with future time-lines and past time-lines, while remaining in the present.

Bibliography

Cousins, David A.
A Handbook for Light Workers.
Barton House (1993).

Meher Baba
God Speaks. The Theme of Creation and its Purpose.
Dodd, Mead & Company (1973).

Meher Baba Discourses.
Sheriar Foundation (1995)

Meher Baba on Inner Life.
Meher Era Publication (1996).

Morton, Charles & Thomas, Ceri L.
The Mystery of the Crystal Skulls.
Harper Collins (1998).

About the Author

Nick Scott-Ram graduated in Natural Sciences (Zoology) at Cambridge University, and went on to complete his PhD in the Philosophy of Science (also at Cambridge). Since a young age he has had a deep interest in meditation, and in developing an insight into our inner world of experience, both from a philosophical perspective and an experiential one. Over the past eight years he has been fortunate enough to work with David Cousins, and to explore different Divine Energy patterns in our world. Since 1997 he has run his own workshops on subjects such as healing energies, the Sixth Root Race and the Crystal Skulls.

He has written two books. The first, *Transformed Cladistics, Taxonomy and Evolution* (Cambridge University Press 1990), is a philosophical evaluation of the relationship between modern classification of animals and evolutionary theory. His second, *Keys to Our Heart. A Prelude to the Sixth Root Race* (LightWork Media 2002), concerns the new energy changes that are impacting upon the Earth today, and the emergence of a new Root Race in human form.

Nick has had over 15 years' experience in the business world, working in senior management positions in the biosciences industry, where he has also written and lectured extensively on a range of business topics, including intellectual property. He has also trained as a cranio-sacral therapist.

Other Books by the Author
Keys to our Heart. A Prelude to the Sixth Root Race
Transformed Cladistics, Taxonomy and Evolution

**Additional Information on Books, Workshops and Other
Activities can be found on the following web-sites:**

www.soulspeaks.co.uk
www.lightworkmedia.com
www.whiteowlwoods.com
www.store144.com